AF522589

HEALTH EDUCATION AND NUTRITION

HEALTH EDUCATION AND NUTRITION

By

Dr. Afshan Anees
Assistant Professor
Department of Education
AMU Centre Kishanganj
Aligarh (U.P.)
(INDIA)

DISCOVERY PUBLISHING HOUSE PVT. LTD.
NEW DELHI-110 002

Published by:

DISCOVERY PUBLISHING HOUSE PVT. LTD.
4383/4B, Ansari Road, Darya Ganj
New Delhi-110 002 (India)
Phone : +91-11-23279245; 23253475; 43596065
E-mail : discoverybooksindia@gmail.com
discoverypublishinghouse@gmail.com
namitwasan9@gmail.com
web : www.discoverypublishinggroup.com

First Edition: **2016**

Reprinted: **2021**

ISBN: 978-93-5056-767-8

Health Education and Nutrition

© Author

All rights reserved. No part of this publication should be reproduced, stored in a retrieval system, or transmitted in any form or by any means: electronic, mechanical, photocopying, recording or otherwise, without the prior written permission of the author and the publisher.

This book has been published in good faith that the material provided by authors is original. Every effort is made to ensure accuracy of material, but the publisher and printer will not be held responsible for any inadvertent error(s). In case of any dispute, all legal matters are to be settled under Delhi jurisdiction only.

Printed at:
Infinity Imaging Systems
Delhi

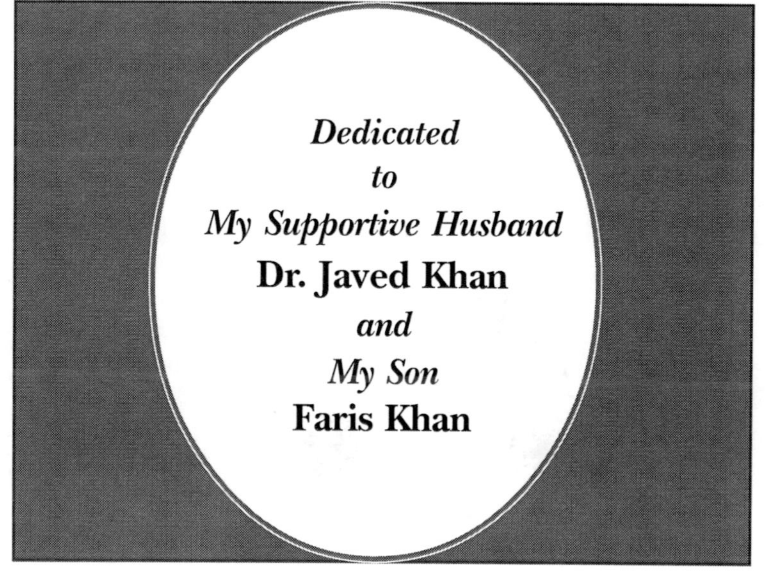
Dedicated
to
My Supportive Husband
Dr. Javed Khan
and
My Son
Faris Khan

Preface

The concept of health includes: physical, mental, emotional and social health. Health education is a professional devoted to the facilitation 'of beneficial and wilful changes in people's behaviour, leading to improvements in their health.

Health education can help ensure that this generation is fit physically, psychologically and socially to assume the difficult tasks of adulthood. Still, the problem remains: when and how should health education is taught in the classroom? How can it be accomplished?

Although there are many ways of defining health education. Unfortunately, health education still suffers from a tack of importance in the school curriculum.

Nutrition is closely inter-linked with health that though good food is one of the crucial factors in ensuring health. This book provides a brief overview of the key topics in the field of 'health education and nutrition'.

This book contains five chapters which highlighted the different aspects of health education and nutrition. In this edition, author incorporates the meaning and importance of health education, and how it inter-related to nutrition. Author also emphasized different body systems and underlined the role and responsibilities of teacher regarding health education.

First of all I would like to thanks the Almighty Allah for the kind benevolence. I am expressing my heartfelt thanks to my mother and mother-in law, and supporting husband. I am indebted to my teacher for their valuable guidance and constant source of inspiration.

I am thankful to my brother, sisters, and brother son-in-laws. In the last but not least I am thankful to all my well-wishers who have given their constant encouragement and support.

However, we do not say that our work is all complete with the publication of this book. So I am thankful Discovery Publishing House Pvt. Ltd., New Delhi.

– Author

Contents

1

Health Education
Concept, Meaning and Importance

CONCEPT OF HEALTH

We are all familiar with the term 'health'. What does his term mean? The concept of health includes: physical, mental, emotional and social health. The world health organization defines health as follows:

"Health is the state of complete physical, mental and social well-being and not merely the absence of disease and infirmity".

This definition tells us that health is a positive state. In other words, health is a state of complete well-being and not just the absence of disease. A person not suffering from any disease and yet may not enjoy complete well-being. There are so many times when we feel tired or exhausted and in capable of concentration on our work. At such times we are not enjoying complete well-being, even though at other times we do. There are other times when we suffer from an infection or periods of ill health. It means no person enjoy full health all the time. However, we call a person healthy if he enjoy good health most of the time.

There are several interesting or diverse definitions for discussion. The first of these is taken from the Report of the President's Committee on Health Education: *'Health education is a process that bridges the gap between health information and health practices.'*

This definition provides a good starting point for a discussion of what health education really is. Certainly a lot of health educators see themselves as bridging the gap between information and practice. A strong point of this definition is its emphasis on process. Health education is above all else a process that bridges gaps. Indeed, it is the stuff that constitutes the gaps that is of greatest interest to the profession.

In 1985 it was reported that the average fourth grader spends only 22 minutes a day in health instruction. Perhaps it is encouraging to think that the elementary school child is receiving at least 22 minutes per day. However, it is important to remember that in the last 20 years topics such as: drug abuse, smoking, heart disease prevention teenage pregnancy, adolescent suicide, stress control, incest heart disease prevention teenage pregnancy, adolescent suicide, stress control, incest, child abuse, ADS, and CPR have been added to an nutrition, disease, mental health, sexuality, personal health, environmental health, first aid, and quackery.

WHAT IS HEALTH EDUCATION?

As with the definition of health, education has taken on new meanings, over the years. Although there are many ways of defining health education the definition of the National Education Association provides a framework for understanding what health education is. From the elementary teacher's perspective, health' education is the process of developing and providing planned learning experiences in such a way as to supply information, change attitudes, and influence behaviour.

Health education can help ensure that this generation is fit physically, psychologically and socially to assume the difficult tasks of adulthood. Still, the problem remains: when and how should health education be taught in the classroom? How can it be accomplished?

Health education that is relevant and motivating for the student requires careful planning.. The quality of Health instruction is reflected in the amount of planning and organization done by the feather. There are many approaches to teaching health. However, the responsibility rests with each teacher to-create and facilitate direct instruction in health and to correlate, other health-related topics whenever the opportunity arises.

Time must be allotted for direct health instruction during the school. There is no substitute for this. However, if the time that can be allotted is can be incorporated into other parts of the curriculum, such as: reading, mathematics, science, geography. Actually, there 'some advantages to integrating a part of health instruction into other subject areas, including opportunities for a significant amount of creativity in leading and teaching.

To accomplish health education, the topic selected must be appropriate to the development level of the third. Health must be taught every semester at every grade level from kindergarten through grade 6. Only in this way can it become a meaningful part of each child's learning experience. 'Meaningful' health education is education that influences a child's decision-making skills. Thus, health instruction must blend information giving with altitudinal experiences.

IMPORTANCE OF HEALTH EDUCATION

Perhaps the best argument for teaching health education is that health behaviours are the most important determinant of health status. Because health-related behaviours are both learned and amenable to change, there is not better time to start formal heals education than in the elementary school years, when the child is more flexible and more apt to accept positive health behaviours. In addition, many of the negative aspects of a lifetime of abuse could be avoided. This avoidance becomes increasingly important with mounting evidence that most health problems are due to smoking, poor nutrition, excess weight, lack of exercise, stress, abuse of drugs and alcohol, and unsafe personal behaviour.

Unfortunately, health education still suffers from a tack of importance in the school curriculum and a lack of adequately trained teachers. If we wish to help prevent many of the conditions that are now the leading causes of death, then we must emphasize prevention in our educational efforts. Children receive nearly 12,000 hours of education in kindergarten through grade 12, yet less than 3 per cent of a child's total schooling is in health. There is only one qualified health educator per 21,500 Students, or one for every 501 schools.

The following is a list of some of the problems of our society faces.

1. More school-age children now die of accidents than of diseases. In 1985, for example, accidents were the leading cause of death in children aged 5 to 14. About 17 per cent of the injuries to children occur, whereas more than half occur in or around the home. In the 1985-86 school years, for every 100 boys of school age there were 51 injuries and 50 days lost from school, and for every 100 girls there were 29 injuries and 22 days lost. Most school injuries occurred during physical education class or interscholastic sports.
2. Nutritional problems, although they have changed in nature, continue to exist, be related children are under nourished. Today's nutrition problems are more likely to be related to over consumption and imbalances in the types and amounts to foods consumed. Many children consume diets high in sugar, fat, and salt, and thus increase their task of becoming obese and of acquiring diabetes, heart disease, hypertension, and other chronic degenerative disease later in life.
3. Vision and hearing problems continue to exist among children and youth. In 1980 state maternal and child health agendas reported that over 25,000 school-age children who received vision screening were found to require treatment. When more than 3,000 high school students were surveyed to determine health needs with which they might want help, the top five were: *(i)* acne; *(ii)* sex education; *(iii)* depression; *(iv)* weight control; and *(v)* relationship. With parents: Physical health problems of adolescents are diabetes, kidney disease, heart disease epilepsy, dental caries and gum disease,

asthma, acne vision problems and scoliosis. However, if we were to look at the death rate among adolescents, we would have a different list. This list would include: accidents, homicides, and suicides as the leading killers of teenagers.

Of all Children in single-parent families headed by a woman, more than 50 per cent are living below the poverty level. Many of these children are at risk for emotional problems, may be less healthy, and lack adequate health care.

4. Surveys have shown that children in low-income families are more likely to be in poor health, lose more school days due to chronic health problems, be hospitalized, and remain in the hospital longer than high-income children.

Child abuse and neglect are increasing. Statistics indicate that about one million children in America are abused and neglected each year. Between 100,000 and 200,000 of these children are physically abused, 60,000 to 100,000 are sexually abused, and remainder are neglected.

In 1986, the U.S. Department of Health and Human Services published Health Promotions Data for its 1990 objectives. Some of the highlights and trends from that publication.

Generaration five of adults eat breakfast every day, 7 to 8 hours of sleep each night. One quarter of men and almost one half of women are attempting to lose weight. Forty-six per cent of women have had a Pap smear test, and 50 per cent have had a breast examination by a health professional. Eighty seven per cent of women reported they know-how to examine their own breasts, but only 33 per cent did more than six times in a year.

- *child safety:* eighty-eight per cent of families with children under 10 years of age have heard of position control centres, with 60 per cent having the telephone number. Ninety-eight per cent of adults with children under 5 knew about using child safety seats.
- *home safety:* forty per cent of homes do not have a working smoke detector. Sixty-five per cent do not know the scalding temperature of water.

- *heart disease:* Three of the principal risk factors for families are more likely to be in poor health, lose more school days due to chronic health problems, be hospitalized, and remain in the hospital longer than high-income children.

In 1986, the U.S. Department of Health and Human Services published Health Promotions Data for its 1990 objectives. Some of the highlights and trends from that publication.

- *stress:* fifty per cent of adults reported moderate stress during the 2 weeks preceding the story.
- *exercise:* fifty per cent of adults exercise on a regular basis, with only 25 per cent, having done so for 5 years or more. The majority of these surveyed were not knowledgeable-regarding the requirements necessary to improve cardiovascular conditioning. In a separate survey done by the Nation Strong Got Association (NSGA), it was report, that in 1987, 23 million people engaged in exercise 2.5 million played basketball, 58 million walked, 24 million ran, 64 million swam, 17 million played tennis, and 23 million played, volleyball.
- *cigarette smoking:* there has been a downward trend in cigarette, smoking since the 1964 Surgeon General Report. Smoking and health. However, 30 per cent of adults still smoke, There smugly, 75 per cent of adults were aware of, the risk factors associated with smoking, namely: emphysema, chronic, bronchitis, art, disease and cancer of the and esophagus.
- *alcohol:* ninety-three per cent of these adults surveyed felt that if drinking alcohol incandesced their chances of getting, cirrhosil of the liver, Only about 33 per cent knew about the association between heavy drinking and cancer of the throat. Ten per cent of adults admitted to having driven when they had too much to drink. Twenty per cent of young adults admitted to having done so.

In 1987 an update of the health problems faced by American students appeared in why school health (AASA). Some of the findings were as follows:

At least third-and perhaps as many as 60 per cent of American youth already exhibit at least one of the primary risk factors for heart disease, the nation's primary killer.

In the past 20 years, the incidence of obesity among teenagers had increased in that same period of time; the incidence of anorexia nervous has doubled. In a 1983-84 test of basic physical fitness, only 36 per cent of American young people aged 6 to 17 met the standard for 'average fitness'.

5. Suicide is the second leading cause of death among 15 to 24 year old.
6. Of the 29 million over age 12 about 12 million are sexually active.
7. Seventy-five per cent of all sexually transmitted diseases are found in the 15 to 24 age group.

Each day, 3,000 girls in the United States become pregnant. Four out of 10 teenage girls will become pregnant sometime before they reach the age of 20 and 50 per cent of teenage mothers drop out of school.

Nearly 25 per cent of young people between the ages of 12 and 17 have a serious drinking problem. More than half of all teenage deaths are related to the use of alcohol or other drugs.

The leading causes of death among Americans including: heart disease, high blood pressure, and cancer – are at least partly related to factors that individuals can learn to control, such as: smoking, diet, weight, and stress.

The American Medical Association found that two thirds of all students have used an illegal drug before they leave high school: 1 in 16 uses alcohol daily.

Both drug use and sexual activity lace adolescents at greater risk for developing 'AIDS and other sexually transmitted diseases not every area of concern in a comprehensive health education has been touched upon here. But it is eaoped that the pressing need for health education has been established.

The scope of health education is a broad one. Personal, family, and community problems must be effectively addressed if we are to live personally and socially satisfying lives.

Many educators share this philosophy. They know that a comprehensive health education programme can provide both immediate and long-term benefits for the children of our country. In terms of monetary costs, Americans spend an average of $1,1000 per person per year on health care. In 1988 this represented 11.1 per cent of the gross national product for the United States. In 1985 $1.6 billion was spent to aid teenage mothers through various government programmes.

Health objectives for the year 2000. The health objectives for the year 2000 are currently being developed. The following list contains some of the recommended objectives that apply to school age children by the year 2000. 25 per cent or more of children and adolescents ages 10 to 17 till participate to more times per week for at least 30 minutes per session in activities requiring 60 per cent or more VO_2 Max.

90 per cent or more of children and adolescents ages 10 to 17 will participate three or more times per week for at least 30 minutes per session in an activity at least as vigorous as a sustained slow walk.

75 per cent or more of children and adolescents ages 10 to 17 years age will participate in daily school physical education programmes.

80 per cent or more of persons 10 years and older will be able to correctly identify the variety, frequency, and duration of exercise thought to promote most effectively cardio respiratory fitness for their age group.

80 per cent or more of persons 1.0 years and older will know that regular physical activity reduces the risk of heart disease, helps maintain appropriate body weight, and reduces the symptoms of depression and anxiety.

Elementary school children are at a point in development-here they are acquiring habits that will remain with them throughout life. It is far easier to acquire desirable patterns of living early either than-to change ingrained habits later in life. The part played by health education holds great potential if early ill life a sense of values, knowledge, and appropriate decision-making skills are developed.

FOUNDATION OF HEALTH EDUCATION

Health education is a professional devoted to the facilitation of beneficial and willful changes in people's behaviour, leading to improvements in their health. The success of any professional in serving its clients depends on the adoption of advances in scientific knowledge and efficient co-ordination with related professions and disciplines. No profession stands alone, least of all health education; in the tradition of the other helping professions – teaching, nursing, medicine, social work – health education is practical and eclectic, drawing as needed on the ideas, theories, and methods of many other fields, but rooted in the basis sciences and in the study of man.

Education

Education is the study and practice of teaching and learning. Health education draws heavily on this foundation for to approach to education practice which includes: curriculum development, teaching theories, educational methods, and evaluation research.

Health education is firmly rooted to public school education in terms of history and legislative mandate. Among the early advocates of school health education were Benjamin Franklin, Horace Mann, and Henry Banard, the fact Commissioner of Education in the United States. Health is one of the seven cardinal principles of public education.

Historically, health education as part of public school curricula has been advocated and supported by numerous group including the national Education Association, the American Council on Education the American Medical Association, and the 1973 White House Conference on Health Education. At least some health instruction is required in all but three states. In sort, health education is an important and integral part of public schools education, and vice versa.

Health education practice in all setting has been profoundly influenced by school health education. Until very recently school health was the major focus of most college and university training programmes for health educators. Health education in public schools offers the unique opportunity to teach health concepts, providing the basic foundation upon which public health programmes can build in later years or other contexts.

Schools provide natural environments for the evaluation of various programmes and of a great many of the published health education research papers. Finally, school teachers, by virtue of their tremendous potential for influencing health behaviour, are important targets for heath education training efforts.

However, because health educators operate in a variety of settings, with various target population, in several difference models, concerned about a range of health problems and behaviours, the profession, training, and consulting as from public education for theory, research, and methods. Furthermore, health educators are important contributors to this literature.

Education, regardless of setting or theoretical orientation, concerns itself with the three domains of: *(i)* learning-cognitive; *(ii)* affective; and *(iii)* psychomotor. Cognition is more, than merely knowing facts. It is includes: comprehending information, applying it to practical situations, analyzing its elements and relationships with other information, synthesizing the information into a plan, and evaluating it in terms of internal and external criteria.

Health education is concerned with methods of presenting information in ways that can be comprehended; applied, analysed, synthesized, and evaluated by the learner.

The affective domain of learning includes: beliefs, attitudes, and values. Affective education attempts to influence learners' beliefs, change their attitudes, and allow them to reveal their values for further self-security. Health education seeks to involve the learner personally in the learning process.

The psychomotor domain of learning is concerned with sills and behaviours. Even complex behaviours can be broken into small units or skills which can be learned relatively easily through demonstration and practice.

Education is concerned with how learning can be achieved in various settings, for a variety of learners, through the most efficient means and useful methods. As such education is foundational to health education practice.

Public Health

Health education has a long history in public practice. Health services administration influences the ways in which health education is organized and administered. Environmental health sciences and population dynamics are the major suppliers of information about the types and magnitudes of problems that require public health education. Bio-statistical methods for information needed to set priorities for programmatic attention.

Epidemiological investigations yield results important to the development of priorities in health promotion and disease prevention; the most important health problems should have the highest priorities for programmatic efforts. Epidemiology also seeks to determine the relative influence elector son theology and resolution of health problems, or practical purposes these factors or determine the relative influence various factors on the ethnology and resolution of health problems.

For practical purposes these factors or determinants can be placed in one of three categories: *(i)* environment public health and medical care; and *(ii)* personal health behaviour and lifestyle. These categories of determinants are also the channels through which health education and other behaviour change approaches are initiated.

Essentially, health education activities can be directed at the individual to influence his or her behaviour and habitual lifestyle, or at public health and medical practitioners to improve care and promote patient and medical practitioners to improve care and promote patient and public health education, or at policy-makers and institute to bring about improvements in the social and physical environment affecting people's health.

The areas of concentration and approaches to the practice of public health provide both the context for health education programmes, and the content and methods for its activities. Traditionally, public health has concerned itself primarily with prevention of disease and its squeal. In modern public health practice health promotion is also included. Health education is an essential component of health promotion and disease prevention programmes.

Health Promotion

Health promotion begins with people who are basically healthy and seeks to develop community and individual measures which can help them adopt lifestyles which maintain and enhance the state of well-being.

The report of the Department of Health, Education, and Welfare Task Force on Prevention defines health promotion in terms of wellness and lifestyle programmes. The report identifies twelve categories of behaviour that are targets of health promotion-activities:

1. Risk management.
2. Enhanced' self-esteem.
3. Smoking.
4. Nutrition.
5. Alcohol use.
6. Habituating drug use.
7. Driving.
8. Exercise.
9. Human sexuality/contraception.
10. Family development.
11. Stress management.
12. Coping/adaptation.

These categories of behaviour or aspects of health are so much a part of the American lifestyle and are so central to health status that any real attempt to improve the health of the population would require attention to them.

Health promotion activities may include policy changes to provide a more facilitative environment as well as health education.

Disease Prevention

Disease prevention begins with an identified threat to health such as: a disease or environmental hazard or a documented risk factor. Prevention is typically divided into three some what overlapping prevention.

Primary prevention includes activities to prevent disease or ill-heath prior to its occurrence. One example of primary prevention is immunizations which are given to prevent communicable disease. Another example is nutrition and fitness programmes which are undertaken to promote general health and to prevent the health to which sedentary lifestyles and poor eating habits contribute.

The more health behaviour is linked to a health problem as a risk factor, the better candidate it is for primary prevention efforts. For example, individuals with excessive caloric, saturated fat, or salt retakes who smoke cigarettes and have high levels of stress are at risk of eventually having high blood pressure heart attacks, strokes, and Other cardiovascular diseases. These persons are prime candidates for primary prevention activities that are aimed at decreasing their risk factors.

In secondary prevention action is taken to enable early detection of a health problem and to stop or modify the severity, or extent of and disease. The dominant activities in secondary prevention are diagnostic and curative; however, prevention of squeal or complications is also included. People with chronic diseases, such as: high blood pressure and diabetes, must take major restorability for their own care.

In addition, people need to know what symptoms should be brought to the attention of a health care provider. Therefore, a patient and public education are vital parts of secondary prevention.

Tertiary prevention is disability limitation or rehabilitation. It includes both medical and educational approaches to help minimize complications and to facilitate optimum rehabilitation once a medical problem has progressed. Lifestyle counselling for post-cardiac patients and patient education about appropriate exercises following stroke are examples of health education at the tertiary prevention stage.

Health education for health promotion for example, is most likely to be practiced in federally mandated programmes in public schools or in the private sector on fee-service basis. Activities are wellness oriented. By contrast-r the role of health education in tertiary prevention is primarily clinic based and patient oriented; activities focus on compliance education and coping or adjustment. Of course, many other activities besides health education are also appropriate and important at each level.

Prevention at all three stages is made up of health protection activities or personal preventive health services or a combination of both. According to the HEW report mentioned above, health protection activities include: regulation and enforcement, voluntary adherence to standards, infectious disease control, and surveillance and monitoring activities. Likely targets for health protection activities include toxic agent control, occupational safety and health, accidents prevention and injury control, fluoridation of water and dental health, and infectious disease control.

Personal preventive health services include things such as: immunizations, screening tests, contraception, and disease specific or risk-specific health education. Likely health targets for preventive services include: among others, high blood pressure, family planning; pregnancy and infant health, immunization, and sexually transmitted disease.

Despite the great need for health promotion and disease prevention activities the total outlay by the federal government for prevention, of which health education is only a small part, is estimated to amount to less than 2 per cent of federal expenditures for health. Increasingly, public health leaders are looking to industry and to local community groups, including schools, to sponsor health promotion and disease prevention activities.

Behavioural Science

Target outcomes of health education efforts invariably include changes in health behaviour; such as one of health education's main foundations is formed by 'the behavioural sciences. Behavioural science, in our interpretation and for our purposes, is concerned with' how 'and while behaves they'd. Contributions from psychology, sociology, and anthropology have provided a substantial, growing body of literature on health behaviour. Of course, human behaviour is too complex to categorize easily.

However, the primary determinants of behaviour that can 'be influenced by education have been identified in behavioural science investigations and theory. These determinants are conveniently organized into three categories: *(i)* psychological predispositions; *(ii)* environmental reinforcement; *(iii)* socio-cultural context.

Psychological predispositions include those characteristics that reside within the individual – knowledge, attitudes, beliefs, skills, experiences, etc., that we typically identify as the focus for educational efforts. Environmental reinforcement occurs primarily in the near and immediate environment at home, school, and work, with relatives, friends, co-workers, and teachers. From a behaviourist point of view reinforcement is the primary influence an behaviourist; reinforcement is perhaps the single most useful educational method, embraced by all theoretical approaches, to education and behaviour change. Socio-cultural context includes the influence of prevailing societal norms of knowledge.

Four broad theoretical orientations which attempt to explain human behaviour are evolving: *(i)* behavieurism; *(ii)* internal psychology; *(iii)* social learning theory, and live social change theory. Each offers a unique interpretation of the relative contributions of the three categories of determinants, mentioned earlier *(i)* psychological predispositions; *(ii)* environmental-reinforcement; and *(iii)* socio-cultural context.

Behaviourism, for example is primarily concerned with environmental effects on behaviour. Behaviourist not deny that psychological dispositions or 'sociocultural conditions maybe important contributors to behaviour, but they feel it is more scientific to concentrate on the 'influence of controlled environmental stimuli on observable behaviour. Naturally, they measure their outcomes strictly in terms of behaviour of behaviour change.

Many other scientists focus primarily on internal cognitive and affective dispositions – knowledge, beliefs, attitudes, and values. They do not deny the importance of the environment, and they are concerned about behaviour, but they are most interest in what goes on inside the person's head. They seek to influence behaviour through mediation of internal dispositions. They measure their outcomes in terms of knowledge gains and changes in beliefs, attitudes, values and self-concept.

Social learning approaches attempt to bridge behaviour and internal psychological disposition theoretic. Our category of social learning theory lumps the somewhat distinct theories of Lewin, Rotte: Rotter *et al.*, and Bandura because all of these theories share the basic common interest in the interplay of individual psychological dispositions and the environment, particularly the social environment. Bandura example adds to the literature the unique concepts of vicarious learning and reciprocal influence of the individual on his environment.

Finally, advocates of social changes approaches are concerned with alternating the conditions of people's lives rather their personal health behaviour. They are interested in changes in institutor, systems, and policies that affect people. They measure their success not only in terms of presents in health, also in terms of improved access to health care, increased income and employment, levels of participation in decision-making process, and other social, economic, and political indices. In this approach, changes in individual knowledge, attitudes and behaviours, brought about by education, are intermediate outcomes.

Within each of these broad theoretical orientations there are several narrower theoretical applications. There are differences, for example, between cognitive and altitudinal categories of learning and change and there are at least several distinct attitude change theories. However, each of these theories comes out of the same tradition of attempting to explain and interpret behaviour based on what goes on inside the individual's head.

It serves our practical purpose to discuss them as the same basic orientation. Aim, as mentioned, our category of social learning theory combines somewhat distinct theories because all these theories share a common interest m the interplay of the individual and his or her social environment. Although by no means the only contribution 8 of the behavioural sciences to health and education, these approaches are essential to health education practice achieving individual responsibility for personal health, which leads to health enhancement, or high level wellness. All this is accomplished through the teacher creating and facilitating learning experiences that develop the child's decision-making ability. With good decision-making skills, the child will make better choices about the personal, family, peer, and social factors that influence his quality of life. An effective school health programme must have a direct influence on children's lives and behaviour. Health education is a life-long process. As a person develops awareness of the many components health and incorporates them into his own life he.

1. Assumes responsibility for his health and health care and participates in the decision-making process.
2. Respects the benefits of medical technology but is not awe of medical equipment and tests. Seeks information regarding health matters. Tries new behaviours and modifies others.
3. Is an active partner with the physician in the decision-making process. Is skeptical of health fads and trends.

Asks questions, seeks evidence, and evaluates information in wellness activities. Examples of such activities include following proper nutrition, not smoking, exercising regularly, abstaining from substance abuse, and effectively dealing with stress. Each person must foster attitudes that improve the quality of life and expand the human potential.

The younger that children begin the life-long process of becoming healthy, the greater the possibility that they will be successful. Teachers must recognize that children bring to schools many values and behaviours. These values represent both the beneficial and the negative aspects of a child's living practices. At the same, teachers should be aware of he powerful influence they exert on the lives of their students. Nowhere in the entire educational spectrum teacher make such an impression as at the elementary level. Consequently, the teacher who exemplifies lifestyle conductive to high level wellness who exhibits a style of living that is physically, socially, and psychologically health enhances the probability that his students will attempt to incorporate those beneficial aspects in their own lives.

AIMS AND OBJECTIVES OF HEATH EDUCATION

The aim of imparting health education to children is mainly to help them develop a sound physique and also to acquaint them with the laws of health, Highlighted below are a few of the objectives of health education:

1. To cultivate the desirable health practices and health practices and health habits.
2. To develop the health attitudes.
3. To appreciate the health programmes undertaken by the school and community and to improve the school and community and to improve the necessary materials for the execution of that programme.
4. To develop health consciousness in the school and in the community.
5. To teach pupils the rules for the preservation and development of their physical, mental and emotional health.
6. To eradicate the diseases through health drive programmes.
7. To combat the superstitions and prejudices in the community.
8. To provide a healthful environment for physical and mental growth.
9. To improve the general conditions of living in the community.
10. To instruct the children and youth so as to conserve and improve their own health.

11. To influence the parents and other adults through the health-educative programme for better habits and attitudes in children.

School Heath Programme

The comprehensive school health programme A total school health programme is needed if the elementary school is to function as an effective institution for promoting high level wellness. A comprehensive school health programme can be divided into three component parts: *(i)* health services; *(ii)* healthful school environment; *(iii)* health instruction.

These three components are outlined. Each component has a planning administration, and evaluation aspect. Adequate planning for all three components ensures the comprehensiveness of each component. Effective leadership co-ordinates the components and ensures proper staffing, budgeting, policy fulfillment, and evaluation.

School Health Service

The basic responsibility for the health of the child lies with the parents, but the school plays an important role sometimes primary sometimes secondary in maintaining the health of each child.

All teachers should be concerned with student health, as any deviation from normal health is a possible deterrent to the ability to learn effectively. Even minor disturbances such as: cold or stomachache can impair a student's ability to concentrate and, therefore, the ability to learn. The primary role of the teacher. In this part of the health programme is in observation, record keeping, referral, and follow up. Teachers cart also become involved in screening the students for various health functions, such as: vision and hearing, it is important opera students for any screening examination they might be taking in the near future. This preparation survives, two purposes. *First*, student anxiety regarding the testing will be reduced if the fear of the unknown and removed. *Second*, the screening exam the a learning experience in; health education for the students. The classroom teacher and school nurse should co-operate in all three apprehensive school health programme. Plasticity the school health services area can these two regional's form a vital team in promoting the child.

School Nurse

In a comprehensive school health plan, the school nurse is most visible in the health devices area. Unfortunately, many school districts have been forced to cut back or under develop the role of school nurses by assigning them each responsibility for gavial schools. This does not allow them sufficient time in a given school to develop the school health service component completely. In other communities, school health services are performed by parents, school secretaries, or some other undertrained person. When schools do employ school nurses, they are either hired directly by the school district or provided by the local health department.

The services provided by school nurses are extremely important to the child's welfare. Most frequently, they provide direct care to, children when they are sick or injured. Important functions are information gathering through assessment of the children, record keeping, and routine assessments. These assessments should help provide for appropriate follow up care and some type of interpretation to the parent.

Nurses are excellent resources. They should be included on any health education curriculum planning committee and should be involved in planning the education of special populations, since passage of Public Law 94-142, the Education of All Handicapped Children Act, the nurse has become increasingly involved in planning the educational programme of the handicapped child. Nurses can assist these children in becoming self-sufficient in the classroom and help alleviate the fears and concerns of the teachers. Finally, the see that emergency :procedures for entries, accidents, and sickness are developed, because there are obvious legal concerns when undertaking aid in any of the these situations. The nurse can help ensure that proper care will be given by helping to develop guidelines are workshops for teachers, aisles and office personnel': in emergency procedures. It is recommended that every teacher find the time to take a basic first course, know CPR, and follow the emergency procedures established by the school district and the nurse.

Areas whether the teacher can be of special assistance in working with the school nurse are as follows.

- *Observation:* The teacher should observe the verbal and non-verbal behaviour of each student for any deviation that might indicate a' health problem. Has a normally outgoing child become withdraw does a child strain to see what is written on the chalkboard? Does a child show under irritability, aggressiveness, or apathy? These are all sings of possible health problems, either physical, psychological, or social.

Teachers are in an excellent position to appraise the health of their students. The teacher sees the child for several hours each day in a variety of situations in the classroom in the cafeteria and on the play ground teachers familiar with the expected growth and development patterns of students are more likely to be objective in their appraisal than someone more closely identified with a student, such as: a parent.

When a child poses a possible threat to the health of the other students, for example, because of a contagious upper respiratory infection, appropriate steps to remove the child from the classroom should be taken. When children are allowed to attend school with contagious diseases, epidemics ensue.

- *Record Keeping:* The teacher should keep an individual card file for each student. This file can be used as a referral source and can also be useful when discussing: specific behaviours with parents of other members of the school health team. Objectivity should be the goal when making card file notes. The teacher should refrain from making value judgments about a child's behaviour or condition and should avoid attempts at diagnosing the student's condition; this is the responsibility of others on the health team. However, school health records for each student should be referred to, because this information could be valuable in understanding the child's behaviour. The health records can also familiarize the teacher with any specific condition, such as: diabetes or epilepsy, that might require emergency care in the classroom. All school personnel must remember at information contained in a student's health records is confidential and should not be shared as public knowledge in the teacher's lounge.

- *Referral:* Upon noticing any detrimental change, in a student's health or behaviour, the teacher should place the child under his care. If a school nurse is not immediately available, the teacher should notify the appropriate member of the administrative staff. The classroom teacher should be able to help the school nurse, physician, or psychologist understand the everyday behaviour of the child. For instance, whereas the physician might see the child in an isolated situation, a teacher can provide input relative to the history of the student's behaviour and explain whether the current behaviour is Usual or represents a drastic change.

Teachers should also be familiar with health related agencies in the community that can provide assistance for specific health problems. This knowledge could be valuable to parents in getting help if they cannot afford the services of a private physician.

- *Follow* up: A dedicated teacher will continue to follow the student's case, even after observation and referral have been completed, if the child is absent from school for any length of time, checking with parents or the school physician concerning the child's health is appropriate. When the student returns to the classroom, the teacher should resume careful observation to aid in the child's recovery.

A good example of the teacher employing observation, record keeping, referral, and follow up is the instance where a teacher observed that a student had recurring injuries on various parts of his body. The teacher carefully noted the injuries in her personal card file of the student. After several weeks of observing, see referred the case to the assistant principal of the school. The teacher, nurse and administrator met with the parents, why described the child as 'accident – proper.' As part of the follow up the school 'nurse reviewed the teacher's anecdotal records on the student. This dedicated teacher, operating within the school health programme, and in co-operation with the school nurse, played a significant part in promoting the health of her student in a difficult situation. She was careful not to make any diagnosis, nor did she accuse the parent of any wrong doing. However, she did keep an accurate file on the student, referred the situation to the proper authority, and followed up the case to its conclusion.

The School Environment

The school and classroom environment should be an outstanding example of health excellence for the student. When school officials demonstrate care in planning and maintaining the school, students learn a valuable health lesson. The teacher can play a critical part in conveying the appropriate message to the students concerning a healthful environment. If teachers demonstrate an interest in the environment, students are more likely to do the same. If teachers are lackadaisical, however, students will share this attitude.

Teachers should require a quality environment in which to work. This is important not only for the teaching-learning process but also for teacher and student morale. Whenever possible, teachers should volunteer as consultants in planning and maintaining the school site and surroundings. Fostering a co-operative relationship with that custom dial staff, lunch room staff, and administrators in charge of the various aspects of the environment is beneficial. Working with the custodians by keeping the classroom sanitary and by diplomatically suggesting improvements can enhance the environment significantly. The lunch room and cafeteria are excellent locations for learning opportunities in nutrition and sanitation.

It is important to teach students the significance of safe, sanitary, and aesthetically pleasing surroundings in which to live and study. This can be done by teaching the proper ways to maintain the school site, such as: treating property with respect and demonstrating good manners in the cafeteria. It is possible to motivate students to enjoy and maintain their school environment. Few teachers are fortunate enough to be able to working ideal situations. However, it is desirable too all that is possible to enhance :the teaching environment. The classroom should physically adequate. Pleasant, attractive, and comfortable for the students. When the classroom setting is bright, lively, and dynamic, morale is improved.

The psychological setting 'is just as important as the physical one, and the teacher is responsible for establishing the emotional tone within the classroom. The overall atmosphere should be one of acceptance, one in which the teacher knows the students well and is sensitive to their individual needs. The classroom should be non-threatening. Stress is reduced when there is a relaxed approach to instruction, one in which there is less emphasis on competition' that pits student against student. Students should feel free to express their feelings honestly without fear of ridicule of rebuke. They should also feel free to fail occasionally without punishment, A teacher can promote student's well-being by being kind but fair in promoting teacher-pupil relationships, setting reasonable goals for each student, praising positive behaviour, challenging students within their capabilities, and tolerating occasional frustration. If they are involved in planning, they will become more interested in the subject matter. Where students are interested are interested, discipline is less likely to become a problem. Discipline problems can be minimized by developing a warm, caring relationship with each pupil and by teaching self, discipline, maturity, and responsibility for one's actions, If is student does misbehave the teacher should that student to analyze his own behaviour, judge behaviour, and choose from among alternatives, the means for changing that behaviour. Teachers should avoid establishing a dangerous psychological set by using school work as punishment: this procedure will encourage a negative attitudes toward learning.

Additional suggestions for creating a pleasing psychological environment include the following:

Although emphasis in this section has been on the classroom environment, there fire other considerations that free part of the healthy school environment. An issue of particular importance is the safety of children when transport of school buses. Guidelines are needed for daily riding of buses, as well as for special occasions, such as: field trips or extracurricular events, Safety in the classroom, the cafeteria, and the gymnasium and on the school yard is an important aspect of a healthy school environment. Finally, the breakfast and lunch programme should be nutritious and appealing to school-age children, These last two areas of concern are sometime difficult for the regular classroom teacher to address, However, all aspects of the comprehensive school health programme are important in order to provide an effective health education programme.

HEALTH INSTRUCTION

Presenting factual information alone "that is, addressing the cognitive aspect of health education – is not enough. Knowledge of facts alone does not lead to changes in behaviour. The failure of so many cognitive drug education programmes in the past is evidence of this. Knowledge must become persortalized if it is to have art effect. This personalization is the affective' aspect of health education.

The American Medical 'Association has pointed out' that efficient health instruction must be *Sequential'* Health should be taught from kindergarten through grade, in a sequence that introduces concepts at appropriate learning levels. The curriculum at each grade should build on what has been learned in previous years and should be the-basis for curricula in future years.

- *Planned:* Health instruction should have stated goals, objectives, activities, and evaluation criteria. It should be given 'scheduled time within the total curriculum', not taught sporadically or used, as a substitute for other subjects.

- *Comprehensive:* Instruction-in only one or "several health, topics in not adequate for an understanding of health. A comprehensive health curriculum includes insinuation in growth and 'development, mental and emotional health, personal and family lifestyles, nutrition, disease prevention and control, safety, drug use and abuse, and consumer and community health. More important than the individual subjects, however, a study of how ail subjects are interrelated and how all affect the quality of life.

4. *Taught by Qualified Health Teachers:* An elementary school teacher requires training to teach health concepts and to relate these to the wellness of the students. Junior and senior high school teachers and school health co-ordinators should be professionally prepared health educators. State departments of education have information grading certification requirements in each state.

The Practice of Health Education

The practice of health education is best discussed in terms of responsibilities and functions. Five broad categories of responsibilities of health educators.

The categories are: *(i)* planning programmes, including the assessment of needs and the development of programme components; *(ii)* implementing programmes; *(iii)* delivering direct health education services; *(iv)* administering programmes; and *(v)* evaluating programmes.

Planning Programmes

The success of any programme depends upon thorough planing. Health education programmes have long suffered from' the tendency to take action, without sufficient planning. The result has too often been wasted effort, lack of success, or inconclusive results. Planning allows for the gathering of baseline data which gives the programme direction and sets up the eventual evaluation.

Planning facilitates the selection of target behaviours and the determinants which influence these behaviours. Furthermore, planning aids in the selection of educational strategies and methods for use in the programme. Planning is not easy or fun it requires discipline and hard work – but there are no short-cuts around planning to successful programme outcomes. There are two parts to the planning process: *(i)* assessing needs; and *(ii)* developing the programme components.

Developing the Programme Components

The needs assessment allows the planners, ever conscious of the practical considerations of how to reach the target population, to develop the programme components.

The behavioural determinants established by means of needs assessment are translated into programme goals and educational objectives. To address the objectives, strategies, interventions, and activities are selected or developed.

The programme components are then organized into a curriculum. The result, then, of development is a document called a curriculum which presents the programme components goals, objectives, strategies, interventions, and activities in a structure format.

Assessing Needs

The process of assessing needs involves the collection of data concerning a population of interest, regarding *(i)* their health problems, needs, and concerns; *(ii)* behaviours related to those health problems, needs, and concerns; and *(iii)* the determinants associated with these health behaviours.

Needs assessments can be highly formal involving surveys, epidemiological investigations, standardized tests, literature searches, and other measures and procedures. They also can be rather informal involving observations, discussions, self-reports of perceived needs, and group consensus development. Data collected in these ways are then analysed to determine areas of greatest need.

Once the data from the needs assessment are analysed, priorities for educational attention must be established. The result of an effective needs assessment is a list of behaviours and their determinates, ordered in terms of priority.

Implementing Programmes

Many health education 'programmes' exists mainly in the form of bulky curricula and planning documents tucked away in filing cabinets. However, any programme exists in real sense only to the degree that it is effectively delivered' to the learner. This process of bringing programmes into reality, termed implementation, is a most challenging task.

It includes staff selection and training; the procurement of facilities, materials, and teaching aids; and the recruitment of learners into the programme. Implementation is a behind-the-scenes activity. It is neither glamorous nor rewarding; however, it is a vital prerequisite to a successful class, course, workshop, or session.

Delivering Direct Health Education Services

The responsibly for which-health educators are best known is the delivery of direct health education services. Health educators serving as teachers, trainers, health counselors, consultants, and community developers are in contact much of the time with specific target audience. As media experts many health educators are responsible for reaching large audiences by selecting, developing, and employing media. These functions – teaching, training, counseling, consulting, community developing, and using media – require many of the same skills and competencies; they differs primarily in terms of the actual process, the identity of the learner, and the nature of the learning situation.

Administering Programmes

Many health educator's primarily responsibility is the administration of various health and health education activities. Most health educators function in some administrative capacities. Aside from the obvious concern with personnel, budget, material resources, and the scheduling of activities, administrative functions of health educators include: *(i)* promoting the programme by preparing reports, preparing budgets and allocating funds, and participating in planning and policy development within the employing organization; and *(ii)* co-ordinating the activities of the programme by providing support for the staff, promoting co-operation and feedback among staff, facilitating the staff activities, and assisting in the conduct of the programme activities.

Evaluating Progress

Evaluation in health education is both an integral function of health education practiced an area of sub-specialization. Some health educators who are especially skilled in research design and statistical analysis as outside evaluators of health education programmes.

Carefully designed health education programme provide measurable outcomes for programme evaluation and feedback for programme revision. There are three basic forms of programme evaluation process evaluation, impact evaluation, and outcome evaluation.

Process evaluation asks the question, "How well is the education addressing the objectives? In order to answer this question, the appropriateness of the learning activities is examined as well as the quality of the delivery of those activities. Methods to perform this assessment include observing the conduct of the learning activities, obtaining feedback from the students, and obtaining feedback from the instructors.

Areas of weakness and areas of strength are pinpointed in order to modify improve the curriculum. In addition, process evaluation provides information useful in the assessment of ultimate programme goals; it enables the evaluator to determine to what extent programme failure was due to inappropriate or poorly conducted learning activities.

Impact evaluation asks the question, 'To what extent were the objectives achieved?' Thus, the focus is on the 'impact' the programme has on the learner in terms of knowledge, attitudes, and skills, The classic example of impact is the test given at the end of a course. Impact evident Jon can identify areas of the curriculum which did not produce an adequate effect on the learners.

In doing so, impact evaluation works hand in hand with process evaluation to pinpoint areas for improvement. In addition, impact evaluation enables evaluator to determine the appropriateness of the educational objectives and, in turn the extent to which programme success or failure is due to achievement of the objectives.

Outcomes evaluation asks the question, were the programme goals achieved? In health education programmes the goals are concerned with health behaviours and with health station order to determine in the goals were met, the earrier can be questioned as to heal behaviours and health status at some time after the completion of the programme type of information is necessary in order to measure the success of the programme and to make decisions as to its continuation.

The three basic farms of evaluation – process, impact, and outcome are interrelated and work in conjunction with each other to private feedback enabling revision of the programme.

- Develop evaluating instruments.
- Perform an educational diagnosis.
- Develop measurable objective.
- Create teaching/learning tools.
- Acknowledge the participants or their contributions.
- Publicize the results.
- Obtain a facility.
- Acquire equipment and materials.
- Publicize the education programme.
- Emi the target population Co-ordinate the outside presenters.
- Provide direct health education service.
- Carry out process and impact evaluation.
- Level the evaluation results back into the programme for remission and improvement.
- Follow up the session with reinforcing activities.
- Perform outcome evaluation.

2

Role of Teacher in Promoting Health Education

Health education has become a focal point during the last few years as our nation has worked toward reaching specific health goals for the citizens of our country. The emphasis on health education has in turn, led to an increased awareness of the need for effective health educators.

In order to be effective, an educator must concentrate not only on academic preparation but also on personal qualifications. Personal qualifications of an equator are important because of the significant emphasis placed on the teacher's behaviour and attitudes. Teaching health is unlike teaching any other topic in the curriculum. However, in health education, the teacher may never know whether a student actually applies a health concept in her life.

Elementary school 'children are so impressionable, and you can teach skills and influence behaviour positively through your own behaviour and attitudes. You have an excellent opportunity to become a good health role model by practicing safe and healthy habits. You must emphasize to students that they cannot become healthy passively. Involving them in active learning opportunities, in which they are allowed to dearly their values and taught how to make a wise decision, will personalize their health education. Your students will be better able to make their own responsible choices for healthful behaviour.

A philosophy that should govern every teacher is the following: Every teacher is a health teacher. That is, every teacher in the school is health teacher, regardless of what discipline she is actually teaching. This implies that regardless of the subject matter you happen to be teaching, you are making an impact on your students through your behaviour. Health education may be the only subject matter in which the teacher must embody the content. You can teach as much by what you do as by what you say in the classroom. In other words, you, as a teacher, are on display before your students, and you have the opportunity to portray a positive health image through your behaviour. For example, if the students observe you eating a good diet in the lunch room, they will see that health, at least that aspect, is important to you; therefore, they are more likely to adopt the same value. You should emphasize positive health behaviour in your own life as well as teach students to make wise decisions about their own health.

THE ROLE OF HEALTH EDUCATOR

The role of the health educator has been subject of considerable discussion and debate. In response several instructive documents have been developed. In a paper entitled 'what is a Public health Educator' distributed by the society for Public health educator, inc., following presents the role and function of the health educator in a clear and succinct fashion.

Why do people suffer from illness that could be prevented? Why do they fail to behave in a way that will promote good health? Why, in short, doesn't everyone use the health knowledge available? These questions concern every health worker.

The health educator, though, is a specialist on the health team who diagnoses these problems, from an educational point of view, and helps to solve them through the selection and use of sound educational methods tailored to particular educational needs.

Sometimes it is simply a lack of information which keeps the public from taking needed action. When this is the case it is the job of the health educator to translate scientific achievements into everyday usable form. Health education of this type is as old as health knowledge, and getting it used.

The health educator helps each health professional do this part of his job better, however, by teaching his colleagues to recognize education needs and potentials in various situations and the effective use of educational methods.

In addition, because the health educator is a specialist in the techniques of getting health facts accepted and used, he works 'closely with all kinds of community groups who are interested in health projects and programmes.

Still, facts alone are not always the answer. The social sciences have clearly that human behaviour is affected by a multitude of forces in addition to knowledge. Applying insights from psychology, sociology, and anthropology, the health educator analyses the reasons people might not be following good health practices and organizes intensive, well planned health education programmes to remedy the problem.

Skills in many fact finding techniques, such as: interviewing, surveys, and community study, helps him in this process.

The people he wants to educate, however, are his most valuable resource, for they, more than anyone else, know what is important to them and why. Then, too, being involved in fact finding is educational in itself. The health educator knows that people learn by thinking through their own problems.

A basic tenet of the public health educator is that final decisions about health practice must be made by the individuals involved. Nevertheless, he accepts a responsibility to provide access to source of information and experience needed by the individual in relating desirable health practices to his motives, goals, aspirations, and values.

The health-educator thus serves as a psychological state setter stimulating people in the community to recognize health problems of which they may be unaware and to work for their solution. Such problems might have to do with pollution of the environment, chronic disease, over-population, drug abuse or any or hundreds of ills which plague our society today.

Depending upon the situation, the health educator is prepared to use very different methods of communication. He is expert in a variety of individual, group, and community educational approaches, as well as knowing which educational media and materials can be used most effectively. Sometimes he helps a group create its own educational materials – an experience which often leads to greater learning than could ever result from exposure to the most polished professional teaching aids.

Sometimes the problems in taking health action lie not with the community, however, but with the people providing health services. The health educator also has an important role to play in helping health personnel plan and deliver health care in ways which the community can and will use.

His skills in education and communication are required just as much to teach professionals how the community feels about health, as to teach the community what professionals know about health.

Health educators, then, are modem pioneers ever seeking new understanding into human, behaviour, new ways to apply this knowledge in solving individual and community health problems.

Another paper developed for a workshop on health education preparation and practice, prevalent assumptions about the role of the health educator and the practice of health education were summarized:

1. Health educators have a body of knowledge and skills to be able to assist people in their own self-care.
   (a) this assumption states that there exists within what is health education both the knowledge and skills to help people to take control of their own life and behaviours, and to realise the goals they set for themselves;
2. Health educators have the skills to help people evaluate possible alternatives for actions which may or may not result in any sub-sequent health-related behaviour change.
   (a) further, this assumption implies that the knowledge and skills for improving health status of individuals are also within what is health education;

3. Health educators have knowledge of behavioural determinants and of strategies to deal with these for any specified element of health-related behaviour.
   (*a*) inherent in this assumption is that health educators deal with health-related behaviour, and to do this must have knowledge of what determines behaviour and of the strategies to deal with any aspect of health-related behaviour;
4. Health educator's evaluation of behavioural determinants and strategies is carried out to affirm whether they lead to or produce specific behaviours.
   (*a*) the purpose of evaluation then is considered to be assess the effectiveness of the planning and implementation of activities designed to accomplish a behavioural objective;
5. Health educators have responsibility for helping people not just to be healthy but to have something to be healthy for, whether or not this relates to health status.
   (*a*) health education has, for some time, apparently defined health as "a state of complete physical, mental and social well-being, not merely the absence of disease" rather than in terms of enabling personal growth and self-actualization as conceived in the definition of high-level wellness;
6. Health educators facilitate, co-ordinate or carry out some or all of the above.
   (*a*) health education can be general or quite specific, and can be carried out on different levels.

The most useful description of the role of health educators is provided by the Role Delineation Project. This project, conducted by the National Centre for Health Education and aided by numerous agencies and individuals, resulted in a detailed analysis of the role of the entry level health educator in terms of responsibilities, functions, skills, and knowledge.

In the final reports on specification, a health educator was defined as "An individual prepared to assist individuals, acting separately or collectively, to make informed decisions regarding matters affecting their personal health and that of others."

Thus defined the health educator may be called upon to discharge a number of different responsibilities and perform a variety of functions which collectively provide a useful description of health education practice.

PERSONAL QUALITIES OF THE HEALTH TEACHER

There are many influences on a child, such as: the media and peer pressure, that may be detrimental. Teachers should be positive role models because they are an important factor in students health behaviour development. Social learning theory supports the premise that educators who model good health behaviour may have a positive impact on their students and may help their students make good choices regarding health behaviour. Students desire positive role models who are honest, sincere, energetic, knowledgeable, and caring. Students desire positive role models who are honest, sincere, energetic, knowledgeable, and caring. Students easily see through superficial qualities.

The following is a list of characteristics and actions that will help you become a quality health educator:

1. Know your self, your motivation and your energy.
2. Be open minded.
3. Be secure; develop your own healthy self-concept so that you will be willing to change and grow and ask for help when you need it.
4. Always look for new ideas and model programmes.
5. Work with goals and objectives be aware of your direction.
6. Keep the curriculum up to date.
7. Be aware that your own lifestyle may be open to public scrutiny.
8. See students as the central focus of your energy, effort, and enthusiasm.
9. Live the curriculum see lessons every days in every newscast, newspaper, relationship, and decision.

RESPONSIBILITY OF THE HEALTH TEACHER

Legal Responsibilities of the Teacher

One of the major concerns of today's teacher has to be *liability.* There is an increased incidence of law suits to compensate students injured as a result of negligence of teachers. Negligence could occur when children are under a teacher's care and supervision, such as: in the classroom on the playground, or when entering or departing buses. Teachers are considered to be acting *in Ioco parentis* when a child is under their supervision. The teacher's primary responsibility is to act responsibly to prevent injury to students; therefore, she should be well aware of first aid and emergency procedures in order to care for a student so as not to aggravate an existing injury or illness. In addition, the teacher should follow her school system's procedure for filling a report for each accident. Each school should have in service preparation of faculty for preventing and handling accidents, as well as an active safety programme.

Working with Students

One of the teacher's responsibilities is counseling students in health related matters. Counseling should be a straight forward and free of moral judgment, preaching, Or scare tactics. In the role of counselor, the teacher must develop good listening and communication skills also, teachers need to show genuine empathy toward a student's problem. There is a positive correlation between teacher empathy, or the ability to envision the student's respective; and student development. When the teacher is highly empathetic, the students tend to develop a more positive attitude toward self and tend to' utilize their abilities more fully in school achievement. Personal interaction between a teacher and her students is critical, and each child should feel free to experience uniqueness. A teacher can help make this possible by accepting the child without qualification.

No matter how concerned a teacher is about a student's problem, she must recognize the limitations of her ability to help. If she cannot provide effective counseling or if she realizes that more help is necessary, she should refer the student to another teacher or an administrator. The student may also require additional guidance beyond the initial crisis counseling the teacher can supply, so teachers should be familiar with available services in the school or community in order to refer the student to the most appropriate one. Most teachers are not a professional trained in counseling, nor are they expected to replace those who are a teacher's personal attributes are as important as her knowledge of the subject.

Working with Special Students

Because of advances in medical technology and prenatal and postnatal care, many children with genetic defects who would have died in an earlier era are now being born and living longer lives. These children, who were once segregated into separate Schools or classrooms, are now main streamed into the public school classrooms. This integration of special students into the regular classrooms resulted from the passage in 1975 of *Public Low 94-142,* the landmark *Educational for All Handicapped Children Act.* The law states that handicapped students have the same rights as all other students and that the education of the children must take place in the least restrictive environment.

The intent of PL 94-142 is to reject the idea of merely Caring for or maintaining handicapped students. It emphasizes prevention and correction. Many special children Still spend most, even all, of their time in a special classroom. These special students bring with them complex physical, social, and psychological health problems. Their chances for optimal and learning's can be impaired if other students do not accept them socially. They can also have a difficult time coping with the emotional challenges of the regular classroom. In some instances other students may ridicule them because of their differences.

Teachers must be aware of these children's special health needs and stress to all students that each of them is unique and that they should strive to coexist with each other regardless of differences. It is very important for teachers to encourage positive behaviour from the special students, by emphasizing what they can do rather than what they cannot do; to find a talent that each student has an encourage development of it to foster that student's feeling of self-worth and to look for every circumstances in which the special student can be included in social activities with other students. The special child should not overprotect or pitied; this will serve only to alienate the child from the other students, hindering social and emotional adjustment. These positive actions will both help special students to adjust to the regular classroom and encourage other students to accept them.

Working with Parents

Teachers should always notify a student's parents when an illness or serious deviation from normal health occurs. School policy should be followed when parents are notified. Some schools require teachers to contact parents through the administrative offices. A good policy is to ensure that a member of the school administration is present at any parent-teacher conference. The third party can clear up any confusion in communication and can serve as an arbitrator in case of misunderstandings. The teacher can explain to the parents the significance of the child's health condition and encourage them to obtain needed care for the child. If a parent asks for guidance in seeking care, a teacher or administrator can refer the person to the proper agency or individual; and one or both should take an active role in following up on any case reported to parents.

Parents have the primary responsibility for monitoring the health of their children, but they may need additional information in order to fulfill this important responsibility. Information about what the child is learning in health education could be sent home a newsletter, which could induce suggestions on how the parents could reinforce the health concepts taught in the classroom. Individualized education programmes (IEPs), which coordinate the efforts of the student, parent, administrator, and teacher in the instruction of the student.

Working with other Teachers

A major responsibility of the health teacher is to keep the other teachers informed of health matters related to the community and students. This information will assist the other faculty members in understanding their students and also help them recognize the need for health education in the school. The educator can represent the faculty on health-related committees of teacher-parent and community organizations and help other faculty members be aware of the environmental conditions in the school that might be unhealthy to the students, staff, and faculty. Teachers should also attempt to become involved in textbook selection committees so that they can look not only for sound, up-to-date content but also eliminate textbooks that propagate stereotypes.

Working with the School Administration

A primary Duty of the educator is to plan the health education curriculum and make recommendations to the administration regarding the health education programme within the school. The teacher can help interpret and implement any State requirement for the health curriculum, and make suggestions concerning the health service programme and health environment. The teacher must also work closely with the school to appropriate health resources. Principals often request that the teacher be included in health-related referrals. The teacher should keep the administration informed about a child's progress in school after returning from an illness.

Working with the School or Clinic Nurse

Because of daily observations of each child in class, the health educator can help the school nurse understand the health behaviour of students and assist the nurse in various aspects of the screening programme by helping conduct preliminary screening in the classroom, preparing students for screening tests to reduce their anxiety, and referring students who are in particular need of screening. Teacher and nurse can co-operate in-service workshops for the other faculty members. Finally, teachers who are properly trained can complement the school's emergency care programme by offering their services when needed.

Working with Outside Agencies

One objective of health educators should be to promote health education and awareness in the community, so they can help volunteer organizations educate the community in health matters. Many of these agencies, such as: the American Heart Association and the American Dental Association have health Curricula and need help to implement their progress in the schools. Through this cooperation, teachers can learn about other health professionals in their community and acquaint themselves with the services offered to students by these agencies.

Also, they should become involved with the local public health department and co-operate with department staff members in providing services to the students and community. Involving with community health council is also important. If there is no health council, health educators can help from one. In such councils, interested health professionals meet regularly to discuss each other problems. Such meetings are not only informational; they also can help professionals solve many problems related to duplication of services. When any two agencies have a similar programme, the two organizations can co-operate in serving the community.

Finally, in this time of budget cuts and termination of health programmes, health educators should lobby, actively for health services and programmes, develop good relationships with individuals who make the decisions that affect health education at the community and state levels, and work with local teacher groups to educate legislators about health matters. Written correspondence helps, but face-to-face contact usually has more impact. Many voices can influence a legislator to introduce or to vote favorably for a bill. Health education professional organizations, such as: the American School Health Association and the Association for the Advancement of Health Education, also lobby on a national level deficient. We do not force upon the child information that he cannot understand or in which he is not interested, but our answer to him, although simple, must be correct, and therefore based upon adequate knowledge. The teacher who is to answer the questions of elementary-school children correctly and within their understanding must be both informed and resourceful knowledge is needed in excess of the facts taught.

The fallacious assumption that non specific knowledge is needed to teach health persists even into the secondary school. Instead of securing a specially trained teacher, many junior-high-school administrators assign hygiene to the teacher who happens to have the lightest load or they distribute the classes among several teachers as a burden that all must share.

An objective test of health knowledge was recently given to a group of teachers in service who were taking a singly course in health education. One young women, who was working in the health field with nature students, came to the instructor after the examination and said, "I cannot answer questions like that and I did not try. I can teach health education, because ! know the rules of the health game, and i can develop pupil activities in connection with them; but I could not answer the questions involving such definite knowledge". This situation is perhaps to be expected at the beginning of the health-education movement, but it should not persist.

The importance of method should not be undervalued, but it will be well to recognize also the importance of teaching facts instead of fallacies. Perhaps we need more emphasis upon factual training in all subjects. From some acquaintance with schools on the continent one gets the impression that a large percentage of American teachers would be in-eligible to teach ion European schools because of lack of training in the subject taught. Some teachers in Europe might be unable to secure certificate for teaching in American schools because they may not have completed a certain required number of semester-hours in the field of method. We should not have top choose between having fallacies presented skillfully and having facts presented so poorly as to be valueless. Sound and authentic textbooks in the hands of the children, suitable reference material and supervision for teachers who are soundly trained in both subject mater and method will promote accurate and dynamic health instruction. It is especially important to provide dignified and scientific instruction at the higher grade levels in order to command the respect of the pupils.

In discussing the preparation of teachers, we shall do well to consider separately the needs of the teachers who are going in to the elementary schools, the junior high schools, and the senior high schools.

BARRIERS TO SUCCESSFUL HEALTH TEACHING

Elementary education majors in most colleges receives very little instruction in health content and in methodology that specifically relates to health instruction. Because the elementary teacher must teach many subjects, most college programmes emphasize methods and materials instead of specific subject areas. This puts the elementary teacher at a distinct disadvantage, because teaching health requires a different methodology than the teaching of other subjects. Teaching content alone is not sufficient health education. Students may be able to pass a paper-and-pencil test on health knowledge, but this does not ensure that the student will put that knowledge into practice. This is known as a *health behaviour gap,* which refers to the discrepancy between personal health knowledge and general health behaviour. For example, the ill effects of cigarette smoking are common knowledge, yet a significant number of Americans continue to smoke. Therefore, health instruction requires an active involvement of the student in the learning process: that is, students must be given opportunities to experience situations in which they focus their values and make decisions regarding health behaviour. Again, this teaching process is no guarantee that every student will make a healthy decision in each case, but it will more effectively help the student learn the concept being taught as well as apply the concept to her lifestyle. To overcome these specific barriers, prospective health educators should take as many courses as possible that emphasize health content and health instruction.

Effective health instruction is hindered by the tremendous wealth of health information. Health education is by its nature interdisciplinary: it borrows form not only educational theory but also many social sciences, such as: psychology and sociology; as well as physical science, biology, and even religion. It is difficult enough for a health education specialist to stay current in health, much less the elementary teacher who must master several other subject areas. This barrier is compounded by the fact that health information is changing constantly the results of new studies related to health information appear virtually every day. The teacher has an obligation to follow these new developments. One way to do this is to attend educational seminars and workshops.

Further, some of the information on health is conflicting in that researchers conducting two studies on the same health topic might reach different conclusions. Some physicians consider mega doses of vitamin C to be the answer to preventing colds, whereas other physicians disagree. Such disagreements between authorities cause a dilemma for the conscientious teacher who wishes to present all the information. Also, the conflicting information can be confusing for the student who is trying to make a wise, informed decision. Another problem surfaces when teachers have to deal with conflicts among authorities or information that is inclusive. For example, there is much information about AIDS that has not yet been discovered, Normally, teachers think it is imperative to know everything in order to command the respect of students, but this will not be possible in situations where even the authorities have not discovered all the answers.

Another barrier to effective health instruction is the fact that so many issues in health education are controversial. Teachers of controversial issues run the risk of offending students and/or parents. Even in some subjects that would not appear controversial, such as: nutrition, the teacher might offend some groups, like: vegetarians, by teaching that servings of meat are recommended for a balanced diet. Further, controversial topics tend to polarize students. The more controversial the topic, the more emotional the students become about the issue. When this occurs, Many times, instructors battle against students negative images of health education. Health educators are sometimes viewed as 'warriors against pleasure,' which means that students think of health educators as those who tell them to quit doing the things they like to do, such as: eating desserts, and to do the things they do not like to do, like exercise. This may translate into negative feelings that the teacher has to overcome, especially when the student perceives that the teacher's ideas are in conflict with those of parents or the peer group. Also, some students come into the health education classroom with preconceived notions, habit, and misconceptions about health information. This misinformation might have come from the home media, older siblings, or peers. Teachers should be very knowledge about them students backgrounds and sub cultural perspectives. Such awareness is critical in understanding a student's behaviour and knowing what will motivative a student. This makes the job of the educator doubling difficult, because she must both provide the correct information and spend much of the time in the classroom dispelling myths that the students bring with them.

Finally, administrators sometimes place a low priority on health education by allowing other activities to substitute for health instruction, or by not placing health education in the curriculum at all. One way to overcome this problem is to help other teaches integrate health education with the 'three Rs.' For example, teachers may use identified health books while teaching reading skills, or they may use nutrition information when teaching math skills.

Professional Preparation

Although standards for professional training of health educators have been set in the past, school health education has been criticized as being ineffective. This is largely the result of poorly prepared teachers. Ideally, a preschool or elementary school health teacher should be a specialist, but this is not feasible when so many subjects have to be taught. Therefore, the elementary teacher is forced to teacher is forced to teach subjects like health with less professional preparation than their secondary colleagues. Some states, such as: California, now that only teachers with a single – subject credential in health, a supplementary authorization in health, or minor in health, can legally teach health in secondary schools. However, the same state requires elementary grade teachers to complete only one health course to obtain a teaching credential, even though they are responsible for teaching a required health course in the elementary grades. Many states still allow teachers with duel certification in health and physical education to teach health at the secondary level and those with general elementary certification to teach health at the elementary level.

There are several reasons for recommending that a teacher of health be a specialist. Health is different from other subjects in that the content comes from a variety of sources and is not limited to one distinct discipline. Also, the behavioural outcomes desired of the student in a health class differ markedly from those with other subjects. Because these outcomes are not easily measured, a health teacher should have specific training in making empirical observations that indicate whether the desired outcomes are being acquired. A course dealing with the personal health of the individual is desirable. In this course, prospective teachers learn more about their own personal behaviour. Further, a base course in first aid and emergency is very helpful. However, when a teacher is fully prepared, for example, in health and physical education, the health portion is typically slighted in favor of the physical education, the health portion is typically slighted in favour of the physical education portion. The reduced number of courses in this dual major hinders effective teacher preparation.

The National Task Force on the Preparation and Practice of Health Educators, Inc., comprised of professionals from several national organizations with an interest in health education, have been working since 1978 to develop a framework of minimum competencies that should be required of health educators. These are intended to guide certifying institutions in the professional preparation of students intending to teach health. This curriculum was developed with a generic health educator in mind, that is, an individual who might be teaching health in a variety of settings, including the school classroom. Eventually

National Council for Accreditation of Teacher Education (NCATE) accreditation of teacher credential programmes in health will require the use of the guidelines specified in this framework.

According to the National Task Force; the prospective health teacher should be sufficiently prepared, through a course of study to be able to:

1. Asses individual and community needs for health education.
2. Plan effective health education programmes.
3. Implement health programmes.
4. Evaluate the effectiveness of health education programmes.
5. Co-ordinate provision of health education services.
6. Act as a resource person of health education.
7. Communicate health and health education needs, concerns, and resources.

As discussed earlier, a teacher's preparation does not end upon receipt of a diploma and teaching certificate. Shecan continue to educate herself by taking graduate courses either in specific content areas or in advanced teaching methods, by joining local, state, regional, and national health education professional organizations such as: the *American School Health Association and the Association for the Advancement of Health Education;* and by attending professional health conferences. Staying current also requires reading up to date textbooks, journals, and other health education publications. Finally, in service workshops that deal with health related topics are extremely valuable.

TRAINING OF HEALTH TEACHERS AT DIFFERENT LEVEL OF SCHOOL

Teachers in the Elementary Schools

The elementary school teacher needs the most extensive training in methods and must be satisfied with the least extensive training in subject matter. He is working at a age levels where the learning rate is rapid, where attitudes and habits are taking shape, and where there is demand for only a limited number of technical facts. In the first three grades the children are held for very little informational material and the teacher's problem is almost entirely one of child training. In grade IV, V, and VI the more progressive schools present health subject matter, but it is necessarily elementary, and the time assigned to hygiene or health classes serves quite as much to orient, support, and clarify the health training programme as it does to give specific information. The teacher in these grades needs a mastery of child psychology, methods of child training, and the ability to develop activities, correlations, and teaching units, together with a sound basic knowledge of physiology, hygiene, and sanitation.

In the teacher training institution the elementary school teacher should have the benefit of:

1. A sound subject-matter course in personal and community health, which will usually be given during the first year of normal training.
2. A through course in health-education methods, which will usually be given during the last year of normal training.
3. An opportunity to observe and participate in a well-organized health programme in the practice school.
4. A programme of healthful living that will make personal health a reality and that will involve health supervision with proper physical examinations, suitable physical activities, and a wholesome environment.

Beyond these minimal essentials we may expect an opportunity for interested individuals to secure additional training in the four-year schools. Some teachers colleges will provide the opportunity to elect course in physics, chemistry, and biology, and they may be able to offer advanced courses in hygiene including nutrition and bacteriology.

Teachers in service who have not had such courses or whose instruction was received some time ago should have an opportunity to take courses in health subject matter and a course in health education methods. New developments are appearing rapidly in both fields, so that such courses, if well organized and dynamic, will contribute markedly to the quality of the health education programme.

In cities having a health-education supervisor there is constant stimulation and teacher training. New courses of study are discussed with teachers by grade groups. New teachers in the system meet with the supervisor for a few periods of instruction and discussion at the beginning of the year. The presentation of health-education material at occasional teachers' meeting shows the various teacher groups the best things being done, both inside the school system and elsewhere, at the several grade levels.

Teachers in the Junior High School

The teachers of health in the junior high school are probably less well prepared for the job of health teaching at present, than the teachers at any other levels, less well prepared, indeed, that the teachers of other subjects in the junior high school. Of course, there are marked exceptions to this statement, but it if fair to say that in most seventh, eighth, and ninth grades health is still being taught by teachers who have had little or no special preparation. Yet it is in these grades that the most define its subject matter relating to physiology, sanitation and hygiene must be presented. The pupil has the curiosity to demand and the ability to comprehend much of the factual basis for health. Furthermore, the subject are departmentalized and the instruction in each must be definite and scientific if it is to command the respect of the pupils of this age.

We may assume that the junior high school teachers of health in the future are to posses a bachelor's degree and that they will have had their major work in the field of health. Probably no other subject makes such serve demands upon the identify background of the teacher, both because of the breadth of the field and because of the continual necessity of knowing many facts that lie behind the answers to apparently simple questions.

The teacher of health for the junior high school needs sound courses in psychology and education, basic instruction in physics, chemistry, and biology, courses in secondary school organization and school-health administration, together with through courses in the health field. The latter should include anatomy, physiology, personal hygiene, nutrition, municipal sanitation, vital statistics, and public health administration. Of course it is not necessary for the teacher to take the specific number of courses suggested above, each bearing the name indicated, but it is desirable for him to have sound knowledge in these respective fields if he is to teach community health and physiology in the seventh and eighth grades in a satisfactory manner, and especially if, in addition, he is to serve as a health counsellor. Such a counsellor organizes, promotes, and inter-relates the health programme in the junior high school, which if successful, must involve the co-operation of many departments and activities outside as well as inside the school.

The teaching of home nursing and child care is becoming compulsory in Grade VIII or IX in an increasing number of school system. This instruction will best be given by a nurse, and preferably by one with through teacher training and good teaching ability.

Teachers in the Senior High School

The duties of the teacher of health in the senior high school cannot be clearly defined, because health-teaching, itself, is not clearly defined at this level. It is seems certain that training in health behaviour should persist throughout school life. It is equally certain that subject matter should be introduced as early as possible since children leave school in over-increasing numbers from grade to grade. Few if any, senior high schools have a course in hygiene continuing through the entire three years. With a properly organized elementary school and junior high school health programme, continuous instruction throughout the senior high school would be unnecessary, unsatisfactory, and impractical. We have already indicated the contribution of other subjects to health education.

We are at present in need of an extension of health service in senior high schools, a co-ordination of health activities, and a better realization of the contributions that various departments can make to pupil health. If these changes lead us to appoint a health counsellor, we shall have a person who will probably teach the course that is offered, but who is more nearly an administrator than a teacher, whose knowledge and ability in .the field of school administration is in constant demand. This individual should be trained as is the hygiene teacher and the health counsellor for the junior high school previously described.

If the health-training and health-instruction pro-gramme is to be effective, it' must be unified progressive, and coordinated with respect to its various phase. To have programmes of that type, some supervision is necessary. The superintendent of schools is responsible for the school health programme and it/its administration there is probably on other factor more important than the proper co-ordination of the work of the great body of classroom teachers with the work of the health specialists. A School administration, therefore, has two responsibilities, so far as health education is concerned:

1. To develop the programme itself in a logical organized, and effective way.
2. To see that the health education programme is properly related to the other health activities in the school system.

The White House Conference took a definite stand or this point. Its report says, in part: 'In the elementary' schools health education should be in charge of the teacher, under the sympathetic guidance of an efficient advisor or supervisor of health education, equinational with special and adequate professional training for this complex task."

It is probable that this definite stand by the White House Conference will accelerate the movement for the appointment of supervisors of directions of health education. In the part such supervisors or directors have come from various professional fields, principally or especially from the field of education, nutrition, physical education, and nursing. In a few cases physicians who have been trained in education as well as in medicine have been supervisors of health education. The success of persons with these different types of basic training certainly argues for the open door policy so far as the source of health-education supervision is concerned. Health education will probably be richer by the contribution of persons from these, varied professional groups than it would be if we should make the mistake of insisting that supervisors must have only one type of training.

In the development of every professional field there is a tendency for the desired training to become more definite and better organized. In health education, as supervisors become more common, we shall know more definitely what the most important elements in training for that position are, and it will then become possible for individuals to approach this field of work more directly.

A brief statement regarding the 'supervisor of health education', as the position is called, in the report of the White House Conference, is as follows: "The supervisor in charge of health instruction should hold a master's degree with a major in health education, should be well trained in the sciences fundamental to health and in modern trends in, supervision and curriculum-building, and should have had at least three years' experience in classroom teaching".

In several schools it is now possible to secure a master's degree or its equivalent, the Certificate in Public Health in the field of health education. The specified requirement in health knowledge for the certificate in Public Health is somewhat more extensive than that ordinarily required for the master's degree.

Training requirements for a health education supervisor are naturally dived into three phases:

1. Training in health.
2. Training in education.
3. Training in school health administration.

Training in Health

There is some danger of underestimating the importance of sound training in health. It is true that complete knowledge without any ability to train and instruct children is of little value. To teach skilfully what is not true is worse than unavailing. Of course, it is absurd to make any comparison between the relative importance of knowledge of the subject and knowledge of educational method. Both are indispensable.

If we are to develop a group of teachers and a school programme for which both the public health profession and the educational profession have respect, and thus secure the respect of the community, we must train people soundly in both the subject matter of health and educational method.

Training in health should include a sufficient knowledge of the structure and function of the human body. This means a basic knowledge of modern physiology, built upon a background of biochemistry, gross and microscopic anatomy, and, if possible, also upon some knowledge of embryology. The individual should also possess a sound knowledge of nutrition, which rests primarily upon chemistry as a basic subject. Knowledge of mental hygiene is also important.

In the public health field, knowledge ought to include general and sanitary bacteriology, the principles of municipal sanitation and public health administration, the biology of communicable diseases, and a sufficient acknowledge of vital statistics 10 allow the individual to interpret and understand the health.

Teaching

Health educator's teacher. As such they are concerned about gathering, interpreting, and disseminating information to those who have a need to know. But teaching is more than disseminating information; teaching is the art and practice of creating learning 'experiences to achieve specific educational objectives.

As such the health educator/teacher is selects appropriate educational objectives, develops appropriate learning activities, and conducts the learning activities to increase the knowledge, influence the attitudes, and/or develop the skills of the target audience."

Training

As a trainer the health educator teachers health professional how to carry out their health education responsibilities. The emphasis on the process of health education and the learners are usually other professionals or staff who are responsible for important health education functions. Examples include teachers, counselors, physicians, nurses, and Peace Corps Volunteers. Training usually, but not always, conducted in short intensive workshops or training courses.

Consulting

As a consultant the health educator serves in an advisory capacity. Employing his or-her knowledge about and experience with planning, implementing, and evaluating health education programmes, the health educator provides consultation to clients on specific health problem, content, processes, or programmes. In some cases the consultant serves primarily as a resource person and information disseminator. Often health educator, with experience in a specific area or setting are sought out as consultants by initiators of new programmes in those areas or settings.

Health educators are frequently hired as consultants to prepare resource materials for projects and programmes in health promotion and disease prevention. Health educators sometimes initiate opportunities for consulting by participating in discussion or planning group. Health educators are equally likely, however, to seek consultation as to provide it, especially from those with expertise in medicine, bio-statics, epidemiology, and other areas.

Counseling

Health counseling is an increasingly important direct service provide by health educators. Nearly every helping professional serves a counseling function and the health educator is no exception. Counselling is a natural extension of the teaching – learning process. It is a process of helping people to learn how to achieve personal growth, improve interpersonal relationships, resolves problems, make decisions, and change behaviour.

Community Organizing

Health educators have traditionally served as community organizers. The goal of community organization is to promote better use, organization, and/or availability of resources. Health educators serving in community organizing capacities are change agents who function in institutional and community settings to facelifting change that is system dependent. As such they seek to alter the social environment it affects people's health, This could mean working to introduce a drop-in centre on a high school campus, or working to remove barriers to health services access in an inner city area, or working to set up a self-care organization in a rural community.

Using Media

There are number of media – channels – including television, radio, newspapers and other print sources, the mail, and locally employed audiovisual aids – through which health educators communicate their messages. In addition Health educators are frequently hired as consultants to prepare resource materials for projects and programmes in health promotion and disease prevention.

Health educators sometimes initiate opportunities for consulting by participating in discussion or planning group. Health educators are equally likely, however, to seek consultation as to provide it, especially from those with expertise in medicine, bio-statics, epidemiology, and other areas.

Counseling

Health counselling is an increasingly important direct service provide by health educators. Nearly every helping professional serves a counselling function and the health educator is no exception. Counselling is a natural extension of the teaching – learning process. It is a process of helping people to learn how to achieve personal growth, improve interpersonal relationships, resolves problems, make decisions, and change behaviour.

Community Organizing

Health educators have traditionally served as community organizers. The goal of community organization is to promote better use, organization, and/or availability of resources. Health educators serving in community organizing capacities are change agents who function in institutional and community settings to facilit and change that is system dependent. As such they seek to alter the social environment aR it affects people's health, This could mean working to introduce a' drop-in centre on a high school campus, or working to remove barriers to health services access in an inner city area, or working to set up a self-care organization in a rural community.

Using Media

There are number of media – channels – including television, radio, newspapers and other print sources, the mail, and locally employed audio-visual aids – through which health educators communicate their messages. In addition the conduct of mass media campaigns has been a responsibility of health educators since the profession's inception.

Such campaigns range from elaborate national television efforts to posters on the walls of local health agencies. Especially as part of a more complex set of interventions, media can be effective in disseminating information, reinforcing previously learned information or existing attitudes, and/or stimulating psychological associations. The long-time fascination of health planners and educators with mass media is due to its potential to reach large numbers of people.

Health educators are frequently involved in the planning, implementation. Nearly every health educator is at times called upon to select or create audio-visual aids and other media materials for use in educational programmes. Media can be an effective channel for a variety of health education messages and has been demonstrated to be successful in large-scale media campaigns. Audiovisual aids are an important part of most health education teaching and training programmes.

3

Food, Nutrition and Health

CONCEPT OF FOOD AND NUTRITION

The word food brings to our mind countess images. Food is associated with worship and divinity with celebration and mourning; with family gatherings and with community feasting. It is closely interwoven with every feature of our existence. This is not surprising because fool plays a crucial role in our lives. It sustains us it nourishes us. It is the 'life-giver'.

This chapter tells you about food and some of its components. It will give you some idea about why food is essential for our survival. You will also be introduced to the terms nutrition and health.

Nutrition is the term used for the scientific study of food and how it is utilized by the body. Eating the proper kinds of food in the right amounts is essential to keep us healthy. In other words, our health is dependent on our eating pattern. This leads us to the vital question-how much and what should one eat to keep healthy? How much and what, for example, should an infant consume? Similarly, how much and what foods should be consumed by a child, an adolescent, an adult or an old person? Further, what happens when one eats too much or too little? These are the types of questions that a study of nutrition helps us answer.

FOOD AND ITS FUNCTIONS

What is food? The term food refers to anything which nourishes the body it would obviously include solids, semi-solids and liquids which can be consumed and which help to sustain the body and keep it healthy. We all know that food is a basic necessity Have you ever wondered why? Food is essential because it contains substances which perform important functions in our body. These essential substances contributed by our food are called nutrients, if these nutrients are not present in our food in sufficient amounts, the result is ill health and in some cases, even death. Food also contains many substances which are non-nutrients *e.g.*, colouring and flavouring substances in food.

Food is, therefore, a complex mixture of different nutrients and non-nutrients.

FUNCTIONS OF FOOD

You are now familiar with the fact that food consists in part of various nutrients. You may be surprised to know that there are over forty essential nutrients which are supplied by the food we eat. These nutrients can be classified into five major categories (based on certain similar features): *(i)* proteins; *(ii)* carbohydrates; *(iii)* fats; *(iv)* vitamins; and *(v)* minerals. Water is important as a nutrient as well as a food.

Each of the nutrient categories has a specific physiological role to play. Here the term 'physiological role' refers to the role of food in maintaining certain specific body functions since food contains nutrients it has physiological functions too, as you will learn in the subsequent paragraph. Food also has social and psychological functions in addition to physiological ones.

Physiological Functions

The physiological functions performed by food are the energy-giving body-building, protective and regulatory functions we need energy every moment of our lives for performing various types of activities such as: sitting, standing, walking and running and performing all our household and other tasks. You may not be a were of it but several activities take place within the body as well *e.g.*, beating of the heart, contraction of the intestines, expansion and contraction of the lungs. Activities performed within the body also require expenditure of energy. The energy-giving function of food is basically performed by two nutrient categories: *(i)* carbohydrates and *(ii)* fats. This is why these nutrients are also referred to as the 'body fuels'. The situation is similar to the burning of coal or wood which are familiar fuels. When these fuels are burnt energy is released in the form of heat and light the fire we observe is in fact, nothing but the conversion of the energy locked up in the fuel to heat energy and light energy. Similarly. Carbohydrates and fats are burnt in the body. The energy that these substances contain is released to perform the various activates that we talked about earlier.

Food is also needed for growth and repair. What is meant by these two terms? As you know, our body is made up of millions of units called calls. When growth takes place new cells are added to the existing ones The existing ones also increase in size. On the other hand, cells do get worn out and did. These cells have to be replaced. This process is called repair. For both growth and repair proteins are necessary. We can understand the role of proteins in growth and development if we just think of the tremendous increase in height and weight that occurs from infancy to adulthood. How does this take place? This is made possible by the process of growth.

The other major physiological functions performed by food are the protective and regulatory functions. Let us take about the meaning of the term 'protective' first. Here protective refers to the role in preventing infection by ensuring proper functioning of the body. Systems responsible for fighting infections. Even if a person dose develop an infection or any other type of illness, food and the nutrients it contains facilitate rapid recovery A person eating a poor diet would take much longer to recover. He would get ill more easily as well.

The regulatory function mentioned earlier fifers to the role of food in controlling body processes. As you are aware several processes take place in the body such as: the beating of the heart maintenance of body temperature and contraction of muscles. Each of these processes in controlled. Our body temperature, temperature, for example, is maintained at 98.4° or 37°C. Similarly, the rate at which the heart beats is also maintained. This is achieved by certain specific nutrients (among other substances) and is illustrative of their regulatory function. Vitamins, minerals, and proteins contribute substantially to both protective and regulatory functions. So does water.

You are also probably aware that several chemical reactions take place in the body. With the aid of these chemical reactions. Simpler substances are used to build more complex ones. Similarly complex substances are broken down into their simpler components shows you sow one two types of simple units join to form complex substances and how complex substances break down into their simpler units. The rate at which these reactions proceed is carefully controlled according to the need of the body. Vitamins minerals and proteins play a major role in controlling these reactions *i.e.,* they act as regulators.

MEANING OF NUTRITION

Nutrition is a scientific discipline with food as the major focus of interest. Nutrition also deals with several other related aspects as the following definitions will illustrate.

The simplest definition of nutrition can be expressed thus: 'the study of what happens to food once it enters the mouth and thereafter.' However, a more detailed definition would be: 'the science of foods the nutrients and other substances therein: their action interaction and balance in relationship to health and disease: the processes by which the organism ingests, digests, absorbs, transports and utilizes nutrients and disposes of their end products. In addition, nutrition must be concerned with the social, economic, cultural and psychological implications of food and eating. "We will now consider each aspect in some detail.

Nutrients: Action Interaction and Balance

Food as you know, contains nutrients as well as substances which are non-nutrients. The body needs each nutrient in specific amounts. Some are needed in relatively larger amounts (the macronutrients) and some in smaller amounts (the micronutrients) But they are all equally essential for our health. Each nutrient plays a significant role in the body. The mineral calcium for example helps build strong bones and teeth. This is the action of calcium. Similarly, other nutrients have their own specific functions as depicted in. To return to the earlier example, bones and teeth also contain another mineral phosphorus, Both calcium and phosphorus must be supplied to the body in the required amounts and proportions to ensure the normal growth of bones and teeth. This means that normal growth of bones and teeth and maintenance of their normal structure and function requires an interaction between these two nutrients.

The concept of balance can also be explained by taking the example of calcium and phosphorus. If the diet contains too much phosphorus, it prevents the body from taking in enough of calcium. This creates an imbalance between calcium and phosphorus and affects the bones and teeth. This imbalance can be corrected by consuming foods that supply the two nutrients in the correct proportions.

In the larger context, the term balance means that the nutrients needed by the body should be provided in the right amount and proportions.

You will learn more about the action, interaction and balance of nutrients in this chapter.

Handling of Food and Nutrients by the Body

How does the body handle food? we take in food through our mouth where it is chewed and then swallowed. It then passes down into the stomach and thereafter into a long coiled, tube like structure called the intestine Since our body cannot utilize food as such it alters its nature and converts it into utilizable forms by many specific actions. This process is called digestion.

Once digestion is completed, several nutrients are available to the body in a form which the body can use them further The process by which nutrients move from the intestine into the blood is referred to a absorption. The blood to all the cells of the body where they are utilized for different functions.

All the substances in the food which the body cannot absorb are thrown out in faeces. The processing and handling by the body of absorbed nutrients results in the formation of certain other substances or by-products. Some of these are harmful and need to be thrown out of the body. This is achieved by transferring them from the blood to the urine. The latter is then thrown out of the body. You will learn more about digestion and absorption in the next unit.

THE CONCEPT OF HEALTH

We are all familiar with the term 'health' what does his term mean? Let us consider the definition of health proposed by the world health Organization (WHO).

"Health is a state of complete physical mental and social well-being and not merely the absence of disease or infirmity".

This definition tells us that health is a positive state. In other words, health is a state of complete well-being and not just the absence of disease. A person may not be suffering from any disease and yet may not enjoy complete well-being. There are so many times when we feel tired or exhausted and incapable of concentrating on our work. At such times we are not enjoying complete well-being, even though at other times lot do there are also times when we suffer from an infection or periods of ill health. This means no person enjoys full health all the time. However we call a person healthy if he or she enjoys good health most of the time.

One dimension which is also gaining prominence is spiritual health. You would notice that this dimension is not mentioned in the definition This is a newer dimension which is gaining recognition though it is still not precisely defined.

Let us now examine each of these different dimensions of health.

Physical Health

The physical dimension of health is familiar to us. When we say a person is healthy. We are generally referring to this aspect physical health is easy to detect and describe A person is physically healthy if he or she looks alert, is responsive energetic and vigorous, lists some of the signs whereby a person in good physical health can be identified.

INTER-RELATIONSHIP BETWEEN NUTRITION AND HEALTH

Nutrition is closely inter-linked with health. If a person eats the right kind of foods in the required amounts, he or she will keep god health provided no other factors intervene. One the other hand a poor eating pattern of eating too little or too much will result in poor health as is depicted.

It must be emphasized however that though good food is one of the crucial factors in ensuring health it is not the only one the food eaten must not only be nutritious but it must be wholesome ad clean and free from harmful germs. If this is not so the person eating the food would get ill even if the food is nutrition's.

Before we go any further. You need to be familiar with the term 'malnutrition' Malnutrition is an impairment of health resulting from a deficiency excess or imbalance of nutrients. In other words, malnutrition refers to both under nutrition and over nutrition. Under nutrition means a deficiency or lack of one or more nutrients and over nutrients means excess of one of more nutrients and over nutrients means excess of one or more nutrients. Both under nutrition and over nutrition resulting ill health.

One prominent example of under nutrition in our country is vitamin A deficiency. When young children do not consume enough vitamin A rich foods, their eyes are affected and ultimately blindness results.

A disease that we easily relate to over nutrition is extreme overweight or obesity. When a person takes in more energy than is able to spend on his daily activities substantially, the person becomes obese.

This section has just introduced you to some aspects of the inter-relationship between nutrition and health. It will be our aim. In this course to tell you more about there and other issues so that you can apply this information in your day-to-day life.

Nutrition may be defined as the science of food and its relationship to health. It is concerned primarily with the part played by nutrients in body growth, development and maintenance.

1. The word *Nutrient* or 'food factor' is used for specific dietary constituents such as: proteins, vitamins and minerals. *Dietetics* is the practical application of the principles of nutrition: it includes the planning of meals for the well and the sick. Good nutrition means "maintaining a nutritional status that enables us to grow well and enjoy good health".
2. The subject of nutrition is very extensive. Since our concern is with community aspects of nutrition, the subject will be dealt with in five sections: *(i)* dietary constituents; *(ii)* nutritional requirements; *(iii)* assessment of nutritional status; *(iv)* nutritional problems in public; and *(v)* health and nutritional programmes – in India.

CLASSIFICATION OF FOODS

There are many ways of classifying foods:

1. Classification by origin
   - *(i)* foods of animal origin;
   - *(ii)* foods of vegetable origin;
2. Classification by chemical composition
   - *(i)* proteins;
   - *(ii)* fats;
   - *(iii)* carbohydrates;
   - *(iv)* vitamins;
   - *(v)* minerals;
3. Classification by predominant function
   - *(i) body-building foods, e.g.,* milk, meat, poultry, fish, eggs, pulses, groundnuts, etc;
   - *(ii) energy-giving foods, e.g.,* cereals, sugars, roots and tubers, fats and oils;
   - *(ii) protective foods, e.g.,* vegetables, fruits, milk;

4. Classification by nutritive value
   (*i*) cereals and millets;
   (*ii*) pulses (legumes);
   (*iii*) vegetables;
   (*iv*) nuts and oilseeds;
   (*v*) fruits;
   (*vi*) animal foods;
   (*vii*) fats and oils;
   (*viii*) sugar and jaggery;
   (*ix*) condiments and spices;
   (*x*) miscellaneous foods.

CONCEPT OF NUTRIENTS AND ITS CLASSIFICATION

Nutrients are organic and inorganic complexes contained in food. There are about 50 different nutrients which are normally supplied through the foods we eat. Each nutrient has specific functions in the body. Most natural foods contain more than one nutrient. These may be divided into:

(*i*) *Macronutrients:* These are Proteins, fats and carbohydrates which are often called 'proximate principles' because they form the main bulk of food. In the Indian dietary, they contribute to the total energy intake in the following proportions.

Proteins	7 to 15%
Fats	10 to 30%
Carbohydrates	65 to 80%

(*ii*) *Micronutrients:* These are vitamins and minerals. They are called micronutrients because they are required in small amounts which may vary from a fraction of a milligram to several grams. A short review of basic facts about these nutrients is given below.

PROTEINS

The word protein by derivation means that which is of first importance, Indeed they are of the greatest importance human nutrition. Proteins are complex organic nitrogenous compounds.

They are composed of carbon hydrogen oxygen, nitrogen and sulphur in varying amounts. Some proteins also contain phosphors and iron and occasionally other elements. Proteins differ from carbohydrates and fats in that they contain nitrogen, this usually amounting to about 16 per cent. Proteins constitute about 20 per cent of the body weight in an adult.

Proteins are the most abundant substances in the human body. Proteins are major components of nearly every cell and have been called the body builders because of their role in developing and repairing bone, muscled, skin, and blood cells.

Proteins are also the key elements of the antibodies that protect us from disease, or enzymes that control chemical activities in the body, and of hormones that transport of iron, oxygen, and nutrients to all body cells and supply another source of energy to cells when fats and carbohydrates are not readily available. In short, adequate amounts of protein in the diet are vital to many body functions and ultimately to survival.

Proteins are made up of smaller units, called amino acids. Some 24 amino acids are stated to be needed by the human body, of which 9 are called *'essential amino acids'* because the body cannot synthesize them in amounts corresponding to its needs, and therefore, they must be obtained from dietary proteins. They are: *(i)* leucine; *(ii)* isoleucine; *(iii)* lysine; *(iv)* methionine; *(v)* phenylalanine; *(vi)* threonine; *(vii)* valine; *(viii)* tryptophan; and *(ix)* histidine. Evidence is now accumulating that histidine is essential even for adults.

Non-essential amino acids include: argenine, asparaginic acid, serine, glutamic acid, proline and giycine. Both essential and non-essential amino acids are needed for synthesis of tissue proteins, the former must be supplied through diet, whereas the latter can be synthesized be the body provided other building blocks are present.

Whenever you consume proteins, your body breaks them down into smaller molecules known as amino acids, which link together like beads in a necklace to form 20 different combinations.

Some of the essential amino acids have important biological functions, *e.g.*, 'formation of niacin from tryptophan; the action of methionine donor of methyl groups for the synthesis of choline, foliates and nucleic acids. There is evidence that cysteine and tyrosine are essential for premature babies. New tissues cannot be formed unless the entire essential amino, acids (EAA) are present in the diet.

Dietary protein that supplies all of the essential amino acids is called complete protein. When we consume foods that are deficient in some of the essential amino acids, the total amount of protein that can be synthesized from the other amino acids is decreased. For protein to be complete, they must also be present in digestive form and in amounts proportional to body requirements.

What about plant sources of protein? Protein from plant sources are often incomplete proteins in that they are less, it is relatively easy for the non-meat-eater to combine plant foods effectively and eat complementary sources of plant protein.

An excellent example of this mutual supplementation process is eating peanut butter on whole-grain bread. Although each of these foods lacks certain essential amino acids, eating them together provides high-quality protein.

Plant sources of protein fall three general categories: *(i)* legumes; *(ii)* grains; and *(iii)* nuts and seeds. Certain vegetables, such as: leafy green vegetables and broccoli, also contribute valuable plant proteins. Mixing two or more foods from each of these categories during the same meal will provide all of he essential amino acids necessary to ensure adequate protein absorption.

People who are not interested in obtaining all of their protein from plants can combine incomplete plant proteins with complete low-fat animal proteins, such as: chicken, fish, turkey, and lean red meat. Low-fat or non-fat cottage cheese, skin milk, egg whites, and nonfat dry-milk all provide high-quality proteins and have few calories and little dietary fat.

You need to eat enough protein, but make sure you do not consume too much. Eating too much protein, particularly animal protein, can place added stress on the liver and kidneys. It also may increase calcium excretion in urine, which can elevate the risk of osteoporosis and bone fractures.

Recently, several low-calorie diets that practically eliminate carbohydrates and focus on eating large quantities of protein have re-emerged in the popular press. Although diets that deviate from a balanced nutritional approach are almost certainly flawed, most won't cause major health threats in otherwise healthy people when used for short periods of time. However, people who have kidney or liver problems or suffer from fluid imbalances or problems should avoid high-protein diets.

A person might need to eat extra protein if he or she is fighting off a serious infection, re-covering from surgery or blood loss, or recovering from bums. In these instances, proteins that are lost to cellular repair need to be replaced. There is considerable controversy over whether someone in high-level physical training needs additional protein to build and repair muscle fibers or whether normal daily requirements should surface.

Although protein deficiency continues to pose threat to the global population, few Americans suffer from protein deficiencies. In fact, the average American consumes more than 100grams of protein daily, and about 70 per cent of this comes from high fat animal flesh and dairy products.

These recommended protein intake for the average man is only 63 grams, and the average woman needs only 50 grams. The typical recommendation is that in a 2,000 calorie diet, about 10 per cent of calories should come from protein, 60 per cent from carbohydrates, and less than 30 per cent from fat. The excess is stored as extra calories, leading to extra fat.

Functions

Proteins are needed by the body for:

(a) Body building, this component is small compared with the maintenance component, except in the very young child and infant.

(*b*) Repair and maintenance of body tissues.

(*c*) Maintenance of osmotic pressure.

(*d*) Synthesis of certain substances like: antibodies, plasma, proteins, haemoglobin, enzymes, hormones and coagulation factors.

Proteins are connected with the immune mechanism of the body. The cell mediated immune response and the bactericidal activity of leucocytes have been found to be lowered in severe forms of protein energy malnutrition Proteins can also supply energy (4 kcal per, one gram) when the calorie intake is inadequate, but this is not their primary function. It is considered wasteful if proteins were used for such a purpose.

Sources

Humans obtain protein from two main dietary sources:

(*i*) *Animal Sources*: proteins of animal origin are found in milk meat eggs cheese fish and fowl. These proteins contain all the essential amino acids' EAA in adequate amounts. Egg proteins are considered to be the best among food proteins because of their high biological value and digestibility. They are used in nutrition studies as a 'reference protein'.

(*ii*) *Vegetable Sources:* Vegetable protein found in pulses (legumes), cereals beans nuts, oil-seed cakes, etc. They are poor in EAA. In developing countries such as: India, cereals and pulses are the main sources of dietary protein because they are cheap, easily available and consumed in bulk.

Supplementary Action of Proteins

Man derives protein not from a single source, but from a variety of food sources, animal and vegetable. Cereal proteins are define in lysine and heroine; and pulse proteins in methionine. These are known as 'limiting amino acids. When four or' more of vegetarian food' are eaten together (as for example, rice-dhal combination in India) their proteins supplement one another and provide a protein comparable to animal protein in respect of EAA. Thus with proper planning, it is possible for a vegetarian to obtain a high grade protein, at low cost, from mixed diets of, cereals, pulses and vegetables. This is known as supplementary action of proteins, and is the basis of counseling people to eat mixed diets.

Protein Metabolism

There are three features of protein metabolism:

(i) Since proteins are not stored in the human body in the way that energy is stored in adipose tissue, they have to be replaced every day.

(ii) The body proteins are constantly being broken down into their constituent amino acids and reused for protein synthesis. The rates of turnover vary from tissue to tissue. The reutilization of amino acids is a major contributory factor to the economy of protein metabolism. The overall rate of turn-over in adult man is equivalent to replacement between 1-2 per cent of body protein each day.

(iii) It is not only the amount of protein that is maintained constant but also the pattern of specific protein in body. For maximum utilization of dietary proteins, the calorie intake should be adequate.

Protein Requirements

It is customary to express protein requirements in terms of body weight. The Indian Council of Medical Research in 1989 recommended 1.0g protein body weight for an Indian adult assuming a NPU of 65 for the dietary 'proteins'.

Carbohydrates

Although the importance of proteins in the body should not be underestimated, it is carbohydrates that supply us with the energy needed to sustain normal daily activity. Long maligned by weight conscious people, carbohydrates cans actually be metabolized more quickly and efficiently than proteins.

The second major component of food is carbohydrate, which is the main source of energy, providing 4 kcals per gram. Carbohydrate is also essential for the oxidation of fats and for the synthesis of certain non-essential amino acids. Carbohydrates are a quick source of energy for the body, being easily converted to glucose, the fuel for the body's cells. These foods also play an important role in the functioning of internal organs, the nervous system, and the muscles.

They are the best fuel for endurance athletics because they provide both an immediate and a time-released energy source as they are digested easily and then consistently metabolized in the bloodstream. For many people, a plate of pasta represents an attractive, healthy alternative to a fatty steak.

There are three main sources of carbohydrate, *viz*; *(i)* starches; *(ii)* sugar; and *(iii)* cellulose. *Starch* is basic to the human diet. It is found in abundance in cereals, roots and tubers. *Sugars* comprise monosaccharides (glucose, fructose and galactose) and disaccharides (sucrose, lactose and maltose). These free sugars are highly water soluble and easily assimilated. Free sugars along with starches constitute a key source of energy. *Cellulose* which is indigestible component of carbohydrate with scarcely any nutritive value, contributes to dietary fibre.

These two major types of carbohydrates: *(i)* simple sugars, which are found primarily in fruits; and *(ii)* complex carbohydrates, which are found in grains, cereals, dark green leafy vegetables, yellow fruits vegetables, and vegetables such as: potatoes. Most of us do not get enough complex carbohydrate in ours daily diets.

A typical American diet contains large amounts of simple sugars. The most common form is glucose. Eventually, the human body converts all types of simple sugars to glucose to provide energy to cells. In its natural form, glucose is sweet and is obtained from substances such as: corn syrup, honey, molasses, vegetables, and berries Glucose and fructose are monosaccharide; that is, contain only one molecule of sugar.

Disaccharide are combinations of two monosaccharide's. Perhaps the best-known example is common granulated table sugar, which consists of a molecule of fructose chemically bonded to a molecule of glucose. Lactose, found in milk and milk products, is another of form of disaccharide, formed by the combination of glucose and galactose. Disaccharides must be broken down into simple sugars before they can be used by the body.

Controlling the amount of sugar in your diet can be difficult because sugar, like: sodium, is often present in food products that you might not expect to contain it. Such diverse items as ketchup, Russian dressing, coffee-mate, and shake h' Bake derive between 30 and 65 per cent of their calories from sugar. Road food labels carefully before purchasing.

Polysaccharides are complex carbohydrates formed by long chains of saccharine. Like disaccharides, they must be broken down into simple sugars before they can be utilized by the body. There are two major forms of complex carbohydrates: *(i)* starches and fibre, or *(ii)* cellulose.

Starches make up the majority of the complex carbohydrate group. Starches in our diets come from flours, breads pasta, potatoes, and related foods. They are stored in body muscles and the liver in a polysaccharide form called glycogen. When the body requires sudden burst of energy, it breaks down glycogen into glucose.

Requirement

The carbohydrate reserve (glycogen) of a human adult is about 500g. This reserve is rapidly exhausted when a man is fasting. If the dietary carbohydrates do not meet the energy needs of the body, protein and glycerol from dietary and endogenous sources are used by the body to maintain glucose homeostasis.

Fats

Fats, another group of basic nutrients, are perhaps the most misunderstood of the body's required energy sources. Fats play a vital role in maintaining healthy skin and hair, insulating body organs against shock, maintaining body temperature, and promoting healthy cell function.

Fats make foods taste better and carry the fat soluble vitamins A, D. E, and K to the cells. They also provide a concentrated form of energy in the absence of sufficient amounts of carbohydrates. If fats perform all these functions, why are we constantly urged to cut back on them? Although moderate consumption of fats is essential to health, over consumption can be dangerous. The most common form of fat circulating in the blood is the triglyceride, which makes about 95 per cent of total body fat. When we consume too many calories, the liver converts the excess into triglyceride, which are stored throughout our bodies. The remaining 5 per cent of body fat is composed of substances such as: cholesterol, which can accumulate on the inner walls of arteries, causing a narrowing of the channel through which blood flows. This build up, called plaque, is a major cause of atherosclerosis.

Fats are solid at 20 deg. C; they are called 'oils' if they are liquid at that temperature. Fats and oils are concentrated sources of energy. They are classified as:

(a) *Simple lipids, e.g.,* triglycerides.

(b) *Compound lipids, e.g.,* phospholipids.

(c) *Derived lipids, e.g.,* cholesterol.

The human body can synthesize triglycerides and cholesterol endogenously. Most of the body fat (99%) in the adipose tissue is in the form of triglycerides. In normal human subjects, adipose tissue constitutes between 10 to 15 per cent of body weight. The accumulation of one kilogram of adipose tissue corresponds to 7700 kcal of energy.

Fatty Acids

Fats yield fatty acids and glycerol on hydrolysis. Fatty acids are divided into saturated fatty acids such as: lauric, palmitic and stearic acids, and unsaturated fatty acids which are further divided into monounsaturated (*e.g.,* oleic acid) and polyunsaturated fatty acids (*e.g.,* linoleic acid). Table 3.1 shows the fatty acid content of different fats.

The polyunsaturated fatty acids are mostly found in vegetable oils, and the saturated fatty acids mainly in animal fats. However, there are exceptions, as for example, coconut and palm oils, although vegetable oils, have an extremely high percentage of saturated fatty acids. On the other hand, fish oils, although they are not vegetable oils, contain poly and mono-unsaturated fatty acids.

Table 3.1: **Fatty acid content of different fats (%)**

Fats	Satuated Fatty Acids	Monoun Sutured Fatty Acid	Polyunsaturated Fatty Acids
Coconut oil (Palm oil)	92	6	2
Cotton seed: oil	46	44	10
Groundnut oil	25	25	50
Safflower oil	19	50	31
Sunfower	10	15	75
Seed oil	8	27	65
Corn oil	8	27	65
Soya bean oil	14	24	62
Butter	60	37	3
Margarine	25	25	50

Essential Fatty Acids

Essential fatty acids are those that cannot be synthesized by humans. They can be derived only from food. The most important essential fatty acid (EFA) is linoleic acid, which serves as a basis for the production of other essential fatty acids (*e.g.*, linolenic and arachidonic acids). Not all polyunsaturated fatty acids are essential fatty acids. Linoleic acid is abundantly found in vegetable oils. The dietary sources of EFA are shown in Table 3.2.

Table 3.2: **Dietary sources of EFA**

Linaoleic Acid	Safflower off Corn oil Sunflower oil Soyabean oil Sesame oil Ground fruit oil Mustard oil Palm oil Coconut oil	73 57 56 51 40 39 15 9 2
Arachidonic Acid	Meat; eggs 0.5-0.3 -milk (fat)	0.4-0.6
Linolenic Acid	Soyabean oil' Leafy greens	7 Varied
Eicosapentaenoic acid	Fish oil	10

Sources

The dietary sources of fats may be classified as:

(a) *Animal Fats:* The major sources of animal fats are ghee, butter, milk, cheese, eggs, and fat of meat and fish. Animal fats with few exceptions like: cod liver oil and sardine oil are mostly saturated fats.

(b) *Vegetable Fats:* Some plants store fat in their seeds, *e.g.*, groundnut, mustard, sesame, coconut, etc. They are sources of vegetable oils.

(c) *Other Sources:* Small quantities of fat (invisible fat) are found in most other foods such as: cereals, pulses, nuts and vegetables. For example, rice carries 3 per cent of fat, wheat 3 per cent, jowar 4 per cent and bajra 6.5 per cent. Large cereal consumption, as in India, provides considerable amounts of 'invisible fat'. Moreover, the body can convert carbohydrate into fat.

Functions

Fats have always been equated with calories. They are high energy foods, providing as much as 9 kcal for every gram. By supplying energy, fats spare proteins from being used for energy. Besides providing energy, fats serve as vehicles for fat soluble vitamins. Fats in the body support viscera such as: heart, kidney and intestine; and fat beneath the skin provides insulation against cold. Without fat, food is limited in palatability.

It is only recently that the 'non-calorie' roles of fats have been discovered. For example vegetable fats are rich sources of essential fatty acids which are needed by the body for growth, for structural integrity of the cell membrane and decreased platelet adhesiveness. Diets rich in EFA have been reported to reduce serum cholesterol and low-density lipoproteins. Polyunsaturated fatty acids are precursors of prostaglandins – a group of compounds, now recognised as 'local hormones'; they play a major role in controlling many of the physiological functions of the body such as: vascular homeostasis, kidney function, acid secretion in stomach, gastro-intestinal motility, lung physiology and reproduction. Cholesterol is essential as a component of membranes and nervous tissue and is a precursor for the synthesis of steroid hormones and bile acids. Thus fats and oils are useful to the body in several ways.

Visible and Invisible Fats

'Visible' fats are those that are separated from their natural source, *e.g.*, ghee (butter) from milk, cooking oils from oil bearing seeds and nuts. It is easy to estimate their intake in the daily diet. 'Invisible' fats are those which are not visible to the naked eye. They are present in almost every article of food, *e.g.*, cereals, pulses, nuts, milk, eggs, etc. It is difficult to estimate their intake. In fact, the major contribution to total fat intake is from invisible sources rather than visible sources (Table 3.3).

Table 3.3: Energy contribution from visible and invisible fats

State	Calories Intake	Fat Intake Grams			Percent as Energy
		Invisible	visible	Total	
Kerala	2140	50.52	3	53.52	22.3
Tamil Nadu	1871	25.96	10	35.96	14.7
Andhra Pradesh	2340	24.22	17	41.22	15.5
Gujarat	2375	32.29	19	51.29	19.8
Orissa	2468	20.73	6	26.73	9.8
U.E.	2115	21.03	4	25.03	10.7

Hydrogenation

When vegetable oils are hydrogenated under conditions of optimum temperature and pressure in the presence of a catalyst, the liquid oils are converted into semi-solid and solid fat. The resulting hydrogenated fat is known as 'vanaspati' or vegetable ghee, which is a popular cooking medium in India.

During the process of hydrogenation, unsaturated fatty acids are converted into saturated acids and the EFA content is drastically reduced. The main advantage of vanaspati is its ghee like consistency and its keeping quality even in hot humid climates. Since vanaspati is lacking in fat-soluble vitamins, it is fortified with vitamins A and D by government regulation to the extent of 2500 IU of vitamin A and 175 IU of vitamin D per 100 grams.

Refined Oils

Refining is usually done by treatment with steam, alkali, etc. Refining and deodorization of raw oils is done mainly to remove the free fatty acids and rancid materials which may be present in them. Refining does not bring about any change in the unsaturated fatty acid content of the oil. It only improves the quality and taste of oils. Refined oils are costly.

Fats and Disease

(a) *Obesity:* A diet, rich in fat, can pose a threat to human health by encouraging obesity. In fat people, adipose tissue may increase up to 30 per cent.

(b) *Phrenoderma:* Deficiency of essential fatty acids in the diet is associated with rough and dry skin, a condition known as phrenoderma or 'toad skin'. This condition is reported in Kerala, Karnataka and Gujarat. It is characterised by horny papular eruptions on the posterior and lateral aspects of limbs and on the back and buttocks. Phrenoderma can be cured rapidly by the administration of linseed or safflower oil which are rich in EFA, along with vitamins of the B-complex group.

(c) *Coronary Heart Disease:* High fat intake (*i.e.*, dietary fat representing 40% or over of the energy supply and containing a high proportion of saturated fats) has been identified as a major risk factor for CHD. Epidemiological studies indicate that LDL and VLDL fractions are atherogenic and HDL exerts a protective effect against the development of atherosclerosis. There is evidence indicating an inverse relationship between EFA intake and CHD mortality.

(d) *Cancer:* In recent years, there has been some evidence that diets high in fat increase the risk of colon cancer and breast cancer.

(e) *Others:* The skin lesions of kwashiorkor and those induced by EFA deficiency are similar. The possible association between the skin lesions of kwashiorkor and EFA deficiency has attracted attention.

Fat Requirements

In developed countries, dietary fats provide 30 to 40 per cent of total energy intake. The WHO Expert committee on Prevention of Coronary Heart Disease has recommended only 20 to 30 per cent of total dietary energy to be provided by fats. At least 50 per cent of fat intake should consist of vegetable oils rich in essential fatty acids. The Indian Council of Medical Research (1989) has recommended a daily intake of not more than 20 per cent of total energy intake through fats.

VITAMINS

Vitamins are a class of organic compounds categorised as essential nutrients. It promotes growth and helps maintain life and health. Every minute of every days, vitamins help maintain nerve and skin, produce blood cells, build bones and teeth, heal wounds and convert food energy to body energy. And they do all of this without adding any calories to your diet. They are required by the body in very small amounts. They fall in the category of micronutrients: Vitamins, do not yield energy but enable the body to Use other nutrients. Since the body is generally unable to synthesize them (at least in sufficient amounts) they must be provided by food. A well balanced diet supplies in most instances the vitamin needs of a healthy person.

Heat and other environmental conditions can destroy vitamins in food. Vitamins can be classified as either fat soluble, meaning that they are absorbed through the intestinal tract with the help of tats, or water soluble, meaning that they are fats soluble; B complex vitamins and vitamin C are water soluble.

Fat soluble vitamins tend to be stored in the body, and toxic accumulations in the liver may cause cirrhosis like: symptoms. Water soluble vitamins are generally excreted and cause few toxicity problems.

Vitamins are divided into two groups: *(i)* fat soluble vitamins, *viz;* vitamins A, D, E and K; and *(ii)* water soluble vitamins, *viz;* vitamins of the B-group and vitamin C. Each vitamin has a specific function to perform and deficiency of any particular vitamin may lead to specific deficiency diseases. For some vitamins (*e.g.*, vitamin E), no deficiency disease is yet known. The minimum intake for the maintenance of health in respect of many of the vitamins has been determined, but the optimum intake remains somewhat speculative.

Vitamin A

'Vitamin A' covers both a pre-formed vitamin, retinol, and a pro-vitamin, beta carotene, some of which is converted to retinol in the intestinal mucosa. The international units (IU) originally established for vitamin A and provitamin were discarded in 1954 and 1956 respectively: 'In 1960, the term 'retinol' was introduced for vitamin A – 1 alcohol (which is available in crystalline form), but most workers prefer the older term vitamin A and the international unit. The international unit (IU) of vitamin A is equivalent to 0.3 microgram of retinol or 0.55 microgram of retionl palmitate.

Some food composition Tables give separate values for retinol and beta-carotene. To convert these into a single value, the term 'retinol equivalent' (RE) has been conventionally adopted.

The conversion can be done in the following way.

1 mcg of retinol	=	1 mcg of RE
1 mcg of B-carotene	=	0.167 mcg of RE
1 mcg of other carotenoids	=	0.084 mcg of RE

Functions

Vitamin A participates in many bodily functions: *(a)* it is indispensable for normal vision. It contributes to the production of retinal pigments which are needed for vision in dim light; *(b)* it is necessary for maintaining the integrity and the normal functioning of glandular and epithelial tissue which lines intestinal, respiratory and urinary tracts as well as the skin and eyes; *(c)* it support growth especially skeletal growth; *(d)* it is anti-infective; there is increased susceptibility to infection and lowered immune response in vitamin A deficiency; *(e)* it may protect against some epithelial cancers such as: bronchial cancers, but the data are not fully consistent. However, the role of vitamin A at the molecular level is not yet known.

Sources

Vitamin A is widely distributed in animal and plant foods – in animal foods as preformed vitamin A (retinol), and in plant foods as provitamins (carotenes).

(a) *Animal Foods:* Foods rich in retinol are liver, eggs, butter, cheese, whole milk, fish and meat. Fish liver oils are the richestnatural sources of retinol (Table 3.4), but they are generally used as nutritional supplements rather than as food sources.

(b) *Plant Foods:* The cheapest source of vitamin A is green leafy vegetables such as: spinach and amaranth which are found in great abundance in nature throughout the year. The darker the green leaves, 'the higher its carotene content. Vitamin A also occurs in most green and yellow fruits and vegetables (*e.g.*, papaya, mango, pumpkin) and in some roots (*e.g.*, carrots). The most important carotenoid is beta-carotene which has the highest vitamin A activity. Carotenes are converted to vitamin A in the small intestine. This action is poorly accomplished in malnourished children and those suffering from diarrhoea.

(c) *Fortified Foods:* Foods fortified with vitamin A (*e.g.*, vanaspati, margarine, milk) can be an important source. Vitamin A content of selected foods is given in Table 3.4.

Table 3.4: Retinol content of selected foods

Retional Equivalents (RE)(Mcg/100g)			
Halibut liver oil	900000	Carrot	1167
Cod liver oil	18000	Spinach	607
Liver, Ox	16500	Amaranth	515
Butter	825	Green leaves	300
Margarine	900	Mango, ripe	313
Cheese	350	Papaya	118
Egg	140	Orange	25
Milk, Cow	38	Tomato	84
Fish	40		

The liver has an enormous capacity, for storing vitamin A, mostly in the from of retinol palmitate. Under normal conditions, a well-fed person has sufficient vitamin A reserves to meet his needs for 6 to 9 months or more. Free retinol is highly active but toxic and is there for transported in the blood stream in combination with retinol-binding protein, which is produced by the liver. In severe protein deficiency, decreased production of retinol-binding protein prevents mobilization of liver retinol reserves.

Deficiency

The signs of vitamin A deficiency are predominantly ocular. They include nightblindness, conjunctival xerosis, Bitot's sports, corneal xerosis and keratomalacia. The term 'xerophthalmia' (dry eye) comprises all the ocular manifestations of vitamin A deficiency ranging from nightblindness to keratomalacia, Given below is a short description of the ocular manifestations.

(a) *Nightblindness:* Lack of vitamin A, first causes nightblindness or inability to see in dim light. The mother herself can detect this condition when her child cannot see in late evenings or find her in a darkened room – Nightblindness is due to impairment in dark adaptation. Unless vitamin A intake is increased, the condition may get worse, especially when children also suffer from diarrhoea and other infections.

(b) *Conjunctival Xerosis*: This is the first clinical sign of vitamin A deficiency. The conjunctival becomes dry and non-wettable. Instead of looking smooth and shiny, it appears muddy and wrinkled. It has been well described as 'emerging like sand banks at receding tide' when the child ceases to cry.

(c) *Bitots Spots:* Bitot's are trian gular, pearly-white or yellowish, foamy spots on the bulbar conjunctiva on either Side of the cornea. They are frequently bilateral. Bitot's spots in young children usually indicate vitamin A deficiency. In older individuals, these spots are often inactive squealed of earlier disease.

(*d*) *Corneal Xerosis*: This stage is particularly serious. The cornea appears dull, dry and non-wettable and eventually opaque. It does not have a moist appearance. In more severe deficiency there may be corneal ulceration. The ulcer may heal heaving a corneal scar which can affect vision.

(*e*) *Keratomalacia:* Keratomalacia liquefaction of the cornea is a grave medical emergency. The cornea (a part or the whole) may become soft and may burst open. The process is a rapid one. If the eye collapses, vision is lost. Keratomalacia is one of the major causes of blindness in India and is frequently associated with protein energy malnutrition.

EXTRA-OCULAR MANIFESTATIONS

These comprise follicular hyperkeratosis, anorexia and growth retardation which have long been recognised. They are non-specific and difficult to quantify. Recent studies seem to indicate that even mild vitamin A deficiency causes an increase in morbidity and mortality due to respiratory and intestinal infection. Deficiency of vitamin A has recently been linked to child mortality.

Treatment

Vitamin A deficiency should be treated urgently. Nearly all of the early stages of xerophthalmia can be reversed by administration of a massive dose (200,000 IU or 110 mg of retinol palmitate) orally on two successive days. All children with cornal ulcers should receive vitamin A Whether or not a deficiency is suspected.

Prevention

Prevention and/or control takes two forms: *(i)* improvement of people's diet so as to ensure a regular and adequate intake of foods rich in vitamin A; and *(ii)* reducing the frequency and severity of contributory factors, *e.g.,* PEM, respiratory tract infections, diarrhoea and measles. Both are long-term measures involving intensive nutrition education of the public and community participation.

Since vitamin A can be stored in the body for 6 to 9 months and liberated slowly, a short-term, simple technology had been evolved by the National Institute of Nutrition at Hyderabad (India) for community – based intervention against nutritional blindness, which has subsequently been adopted by other countries. The strategy is to administer a single massive dose of 200,000 IU of vitamin A in oil (retinol palmitate.) orally every 6 months to pre-school children (1 year to 6 year), and half that dose (100,00 IU) to children between 6 months and one year of age. In this way, the child would be, as it were 'immunized' against xerophthalmia. The protection afforded by six-monthly dosing seems very adequate as measured by clinical signs of deficiency . In a longitudinal study in Hyderabad city, the incidence of keratomalacia in areas covered by the programme decreased by about 80 per cent.

Assessment of Vitamin A Deficiency

The formulation of an effective intervention programme for prevention of vitamin A deficiency (VAD) begins with the characterization of the problem. This is done by population surveys employing both clinical and biochemical criteria. These surveys (prevalence surveys) are done on preschool children (6 months to 6 years) who are at special risk. The Criteria recommended by WHO are given in Table 3.5. The presence of any one of the criteria should be considered as evidence of a xerophthalmia problem in the community.

Table 3.5: Prevalence criteria for determining the xerophthalmia problem

Night blindness	More than 1%
Bitot's spt	More than 0.5%
Corneal xerosis/corneal	More than 0.01%
Ulceration/keratomalacia	
Corneal ulcer	More than 0.005%
Serum retinol (less than 10 mcg/dl)	More than 5%

Vitamin A deficiency in India: Vitamin A deficiency is considered a public health problem in India. The nation-wide 'survey of blindness conducted during 1986-89, included the prevalence of vitamin A deficiency in children. The prevalence rate of 6.01 per cent in children under 6 years of age was recorded, although there was a wide range of variations between the States. The prevalence rate of vitamin A deficiency state-wise is given in Table 3.6.

Table 3.6: Prevalence rate of vitamin A deficiency 0-6 years

Kerala, Meghalaya; Sikkim,
Andhra Pradesh, Karnataka, Manipur, Orissa, Punjab, Chandigarh, Lakshadweep, 'Mizoram.
Haryana Himachal Pradesh J&K Maharashtra, Nagaland, Tamil Nadu, Arunachal Pradesh, Delhi, Goa, Pondicherry.
Assam Bihar Gujarat, 'Madhya Pradesh, Rajasthan, Tripura Uttar Pradesh, West Bengal, and Nicobar Islands.

There are indications of declining trends of vitamin A deficiency. In a nation-wide survey of the prevalence and cause of blindness during 1971-74, VAD accounted for 0.3 per cent of the total cause of blindness in the country. The proportion has declined to 0.04 per cent in a similar survey during 1986-89. Number of keratomalacia has declined significantly. Repeat surveys (1975-79 and 1988-90) by the National Nutrition Monitoring Bureau in Andhra Pradesh, Gujarat, Karnataka, Kerala, Madhya Pradesh, Maharashtra, Orissa and Tamil Nadu, documented a decline of overall prevalence rate of Bitot's spots from 1.8 per cent to 07 per cent, Vitamin A administration to children 9 month to 3 years of age has been included in the CSSM programme.

Recommended Allowances

The recommended daily intake of vitamin A is 600 micrograms for adults. The detailed recommendations are given in Table 3.7.

Toxicity

An excess intake of retinol causes nausea, vomiting, anorexia and sleep disorders followed by skin desquamation and then an enlarged liver and papillary oedema. High intakes of carotene may colour plasma and skin, but do not appear to be dangerous (25, 34). The teratogenic effects of massive doses of vitamin A are the most recent focus of interest.

Table 3.7: **Daily intake of vitamin a recommended by ICMR (1989)**

Group	Rating (Mcg)	B-Carotine (Mcg)
Adults		
Man	600	2400
Woman	600	2400
Pregnancy	600	2400
Lactation	950	3800
Infants 0 to 12 year	350	1200
Children 1 to 6 years 7 to 12 years	400 600	1600 2400
Adolescents 13 to 19 years	600	2400

VITAMIN D

The nutritionally important forms of Vitamin D in man are Calceferol (Vitamin D2) and Cholecalciferol (Vitamin D 3). Calciferol may be derived by irradiation of the plant sterol, ergosterol. Cholecalciferol is the naturally occurring (preformed) vitamin D which is found in animal fats and fish liver oils. It is also derived from exposure to UV rays of the sunlight which convert the cholesterol in the skin to vitamin D. Vitamin D is stored largely in the fat depots.

Vitamin D: Kidney Hormone

Major advances have been made in recent years in our understanding of the metabolism of vitamin D in the body. It is now known that vitamin D, by itself, is metabolically inactive unless it undergoes endogenous transformation into several active metabolites (*e.g.*, 25, HCC; 1:25 DHCC) first in the liver and later in the kidney. These metabolites are bound to specific transport proteins and are carried to the target tissues – bone and intestine. It has been proposed that vitamin D should be regarded as a kidney hormone because it does not meet the classic definition of a vitamin, that is, a substance which must be obtained by dietary means because of a lack of capacity in the human body to synthesize it. In fact, vitamin D is not a dietary requirement at all in conditions of adequate sunlight. It can be synthesized in the body in adequate amounts by simple exposure to sunlight even for 5 minutes per day.

Functions

Functions of vitamin D and its metabolites:

Intestine : Promutes intestinal absorption of calcium and phosphorus.

Bone : Stimulates normal mineralization Enhances bone resorption Affects collagen maturation.

Kidney : Increases tubular reabsorption of phosphate Variable effect on reabsorption of calcium.

Other : Permits normal growth.

Sources

Vitamin D is unique because it is derived both form sunlight and foods. *(a)* Sunlight: Vitamin D is synthesized by the body by the action of UV rays of sunlight on 7-dehydrocholesterol, which is stored in large abundance in the skin, Exposure to UV rays is critical; these can be filtered off by air pollution. Dark – skinned races such as: Negroes also suffer from this disadvantage because black skin can filter off up to 95 per cent of UV rays. *(b) Foods:* Vitamin D occurs only in foods of animal origin. Liver, egg yolk, butter and cheese and some species of fish contain useful amounts. Fish liver oils, although not considered to be a food, are the richest source of vitamin D. Human milk has recently been shown to contain considerable amounts of water – soluble, vitamin D *sulphate.* Other sources of vitamin D are foods artificially fortified with vitamin D, such as: milk, margarine, vanaspati and infant foods. Dietary source of vitamin D are given in Table 3.8.

Table 3.8: Dietary sources of vitamin D

	Ug/per 100g		Ug/per 100g
Butter	0.5-1.5	Shark liver oil	30-100
Eggs	1.25-1.5	Cod liver oil	200-750
Milk, whole	0.1	Halibut liver oil	500-10,000
Fish fat	5-30		

Deficiency

1. *Rickets*: Vitamin D deficiency leads to *rickets*, which is usually observed in young children between the age of six months and two years. There is reduced calcification of growing bones. The disease is characterised by growth failure, bone deformity, muscular hypertonia, tetany and convulsions due to hypo-calcemia. There is an elevated concentration of alkaline phosphate in the serum. The bony deformities include curved legs, deformed pelvis, pigeon chest, Harrison's sulcus, rickets rosary, etc. The milestones of development such as: walking and teething are delayed.
2. *Osteomalacia:* In adults, vitamin D deficiency may result in osteomalacia which occurs mainly in women, especially during pregnancy and lactation when requirements of vitamin D are increased.

Both rickets and osteomaiacia are frequently reported in India, although they do not appear to be a problem of public health importance. In the world as a whole, their prevalence has declined as a result of changes in social customs, and the expansion of mother and child health service leading to better care and feeding of infants and children. In the developing countries today, rickets as a menace to health is overshadowed by the prevalence of protein malnutrition.

Prevention

Prevention measures include: *(a)* educating parents to experience their children regularly to sunshine; *(b)* periodic (prophylaxis) of young children with vitamin D; and *(c)* Vitamin D fortification of foods, especially milk. Some industrialised countries still carry out the last measure. Periodic dosing and education appear to be the most practical approaches in developing countries.

Fraser urges caution concerning oral supplementation, because orally administered vitamin D appears to bypass the protective mechanism that prevent excessive 25 (OH) D3 formation. The margin of safety with oral vitamin D between the nutrient requirement and toxic intake is narrow.

Vitamin D is stored in the body in fatty tissues and in the liver. An excessive intake is harmful and may result in anorexia, nausea, vomiting, thirst, and drowsiness. The patient may lapse into coma, while cardiac arrhythmias and renal failure may occur. The effects are due to hypercalcemia induced by increased intestinal absorption and mobilization of calcium from bone. Recent literature contains warning against the administration of amounts of vitamin D that greatly exceed accepted requirement levels. This warning applies to pregnant women also since manifestations of hypercalcemia may develop in uterus.

Daily Requirements

The daily requirements of vitamin D are:

Adults	2.5 mcg (100 IU)
Infants and children	5.0 mcg (200 IU)
Pregnancy and lactation	10.0 mcg (400 IU)

(One international unit (IU) of vitamin D = 0.025 g of calciferol – that is, to convert IU to micrograms, divide by 40).

VITAMIN E

(Tocopherol)

Vitamin E is the generic name for a group of closely related and naturally occurring fat soluble compounds, the tocopherols. Of these alpha-tocopherol is biologically the most potent. Vitamin E is widely distributed in foods. By far the richest sources are vegetable oils, cotton-seed, sunflower seed, egg yolk and butter. Foods rich in polyunsaturated fatty acids are also rich in vitamin E. The usual plasma level of vitamin E in adults is between 0.8 and 1.4 mg per 100 mi. While there is no doubt that man requires tocopherol in his diet, there is no clear indication of dietary deficiency. The role of vitamin E at the molecular level is little understood. The current estimate of vitamin E requirement is about 0.8 mg/g of essential fatty acids.

Recently the cytotoxic effect of vitamin E on human lymphocytes *in vitro* at high concentrations has been reported. This being so, caution should be exercised against the mega-dose consumption of vitamin E in clinical practice.

VITAMIN K

Vitamin K occurs in at least two major forms – vitamin K_1 and vitamin K_2. Vitamin Kt is found mainly in fresh green vegetables particularly dark green ones, and in some fruits. Cow's milk is a richer source (60 mcg/L) of vitamin K than human milk (15 mcg/L). Vitamin K_2 is synthesized by the intestinal bacteria, which usually provide an adequate supply in man. Long-term administration of antibiotic doses for more than a week may temporarily suppress the normal intestinal flora, (a source of vitamin K_2) and may cause a deficiency of vitamin K. Vitamin K is stored in the liver.

The role of vitamin K is to stimulate the production and/or the release of certain coagulation factors. In vitamin K deficiency, the prothrombin content of blood is markedly decreased and the blood clotting time is considerably prolonged. The vitamin K requirement of man is met by a combination of dietary intake and microbial synthesis in the gut. The daily requirement for man appears to be about 0.03 mg/kg for the adult. Newborn infants tend to be deficient in vitamin K due to minimal stores of prothrombin at birth and lack of an established intestinal flora. Soon after birth, all infants or those at increased risk should receive a single intramuscular dose of a vitamin K preparation (0.1-0.2mg of menadione sodium bisulphite or 0.5 mg of vitamin K_1) by way of prophylaxis.

THIAMINE

Thiamine (vitamin B1) is a water-soluble vitamin. It is essential for the utilization of carbohydrates. Thiamine pyrophosphate (TPP), the coenzyme of cocarboxylase plays a part in activating transketolase, an enzyme involved in the direct oxidative pathway for glucose. In thiamine deficiency, there is accumulation of pyruvic and lactic acids in the tissues and body fluids.

Sources

Thiamine occurs in all natural foods, although in small amounts. Important sources are: whole grain cereals, wheat, gram, yeast, pulses, oilseeds and nuts, especially groundnut.

Meat, fish, eggs, vegetables and fruits contain smaller amounts. Milk is an important source of thiamine for infants, provided the thiamine status of their mothers is satisfactory. The main source of thiamine in the diet of Indian people is cereals (rice and wheat) which contribute from 60-85 per cent of the total supply. The thiamine content of selected food stuff is given in Table 3.9.

Table 3.9: Dietary sources of thiamine

Wheat whole	0.45	Milk, cows	0.05
Rice raw, home pounded	0.21	Egg. hen's	0.10
Rice, milled	0.06	Mutton	0.18
Bengal gram dhal	0.24	Liver, Sheep	0.36
Almonds	0.24		
Gingelly seeds	1.01		
Groundnut	0.90		

Source

Thiamine Losses

Thiamine is readily lost from rice during the process of milling. Being a water soluble vitamin, further losses take place during washing and cooking of rice. This is the basis for advising people to eschew highly polished rice and eat parboiled or under-milled rice. Much of thiamine in fruits and vegetables is generally lost during prolonged storage. Thiamine is also destroyed in toast and in cereals cooked with baking soda. The occurrence or absence of beriberi is determined by the local customs and cultural practices concerning the processing and cooking of rice and other foodstuffs.

Deficiency

The two principal deficiency diseases are: beriberi and Wernick's encephalopathy. Beriberi may occur in three main forms:

(i) The dry form characterised by nerve involvement (peripheral neuritis).

(ii) The wet form characterised by heart involvement (cardiac beri-beri).

(iii) Infantile beriberi, seen in infants between 2 and 4 months of age. The affected baby is usually breast-fed by a thiamine-deficient mother who commonly shows signs of peripheral neuropathy. Wernicke's encephalopathy (seen often in alcoholics) is characterised by ophthalmoplegia polyneuritis, ataxia and mental deterioration.

It occurs occasionally in people who fast.

A few Short decades ago, frank cases of beriberi used to be frequently seen in the coastal districts of Andhra Pradesh where people eat highly polished rice. Recent investigations by the ICMR showed that such cases are now rarely encountered because of improved socio-economic conditions and diversification in the diet consumed now. However, manifestations of minor degrees of thiamine deficiency such as: loss of appetite, absence of ankle and knee jerks, and presence of calf tenderness have been frequently encountered in nutrition.

Surveys indicating that the disease remains endemic in a moderate or mild form among certain sections of the population. In the Western countries, beriberi does occur occasionally and is most commonly due to excessive alcohol consumption.

Prevention

Beriberi can be eliminated by educating people to eat well-balanced, mixed diets containing thiamine-rich foods (*e.g.*, parboiled and undermilled rice) and to stop all alcohol. Direct supplementation of high-risk groups (*e.g.*, lactating mothers) is another approach. Beriberi tends to disappear as economic conditions improve and diets become more varied. The disease, as has been shown, is not completely vanquished but the knowledge and resources needed to bring about its disappearance are available.

Recommended Allowances

Daily requirement of thiamine is 0.5 mg per 1000 kcals of energy intake. The body content of thiamine is placed at 30mg, and if more than this is given it is merely lost in the urine. Patients on regular haemodialysis should routinely be 'given supplements of thiamine. Thiamine should also be given prophylactically to people with persistent vomiting or prolonged gastric aspiration and those who go on long fasts. For further details see Table 3.10.

RIBOFLAVIN

Riboflavin (Vitamin B2) is a member of the B-group vitamins. It has a fundamental role in cellular oxidation. It is a co-factor in number of enzymes involved with energy metabolism.

Sources

Its richest natural sources are: milk, eggs, liver, kidney and green leafy vegetables. Meat and fish contain small amounts. Cereals (whether whole or milled) and pulses are relatively poor sources but because of the bulk in which they are consumed, they contribute much of the riboflavin to Indian diets. Germination increases the riboflavin content of pulses and cereals. The riboflavin content of some common foods is given in Table 3.10.

Table 3.10: Dietary sources of riboflavin

Foods of Vegetable Origin	mg/100g	Foods of Animal Origin	mg/100g
Liver, sheep	1.70	Whole cereals	0.10-0.16
Milk, cow's	0.19	Milled cereals	
Egg, hen	0.40	Pulses	
Meat	0.14	Leafy veg	

Deficiency

Deficiency of riboflavin, or ariboflavinosis is widespread in India particularly in population where rice is the staple. The most common lesion associated with riboflavin deficiency is angular stomatitis, which occurs frequently in malnourished children and its prevalence is used as an index of the state of nutrition of groups of children. Other clinical signs suggestive (but not specific) include cheilosis, glossitis, nasolabial dyssebacia, etc. Studies conducted at National Institute of Nutrition in India showed that subclinical riboflavin deficiency (as judged by the erythrocyte glutathione reductive activation test) was present in over 80 per cent of low income group children and adults. Hypo-ribofiavinosis, even when severe, seldom incapacitates the individual, but it may have subtle functional effects such as: impaired neuromata function, wound healing and perhaps increased susceptibility to cataract. Riboflavin deficiency almost always occurs in association with deficiencies of other B-complex vitamins such as: pyridoxine; it is usually a part of a multiple deficiency syndrome.

Requirement

There are no real body stores of riboflavin. Daily requirement is 0.6mg per 1000kcal of energy intake.

NIACIN

Niacin or nicotinic acid is essential for the metabolism of carbohydrate, fat and protein. It is also essential for the normal functioning of the skin, intestinal and nervous systems. This vitamin differs from the other vitamins of the B-complex group in that an essential amino acid, tryptophan serves as its precursor. Another characteristic of niacin is that it is not excreted in urine as such, but is metabolised to at least 2 major methylated derivatives: *(i)* N-methyl-nicotinamide; and *(ii)* N-methyl pyridones.

Sources

Foods rich in niacin and/or tryptophan are liver, kidney meat, poultry, fish, legumes and groundnut. Milk is a poor source of niacin but its proteins are rich in tryptophan which is converted in the body into niacin (about 60 mg of tryptophan is required to result in 1 mg of niacin). In many cereals, especially maize, niacin occurs in 'bound' form unavailable to the consumer.

Deficiency

Niacin deficiency results in pellagra. The disease is characterised by three D's: *(i)* diarrhoea; *(ii)* dermatitis; and *(iii)* dementia. In addition glossitis and stomatitis usually occur. The dermatitis is bilaterally symmetrical and is found only on those surfaces of the body exposed to sunlight, such as: back of the hands, lower legs, face and neck. Mental changes may also occur which include depression, irritability and delirium.

Once a formidable and widespread deficiency disease among malnourished population subsisting mainly on maize diets, pellagra has declined in all parts of the world. It is still prevalent in some parts of Western Asia and Southern Africa where people subsist on maize and little else. While pellagra is historically a disease of the maize-eating population, it has been reported in India in the Telangana area of Andhra Pradesh in some segments of the population eating another cereal – that is jowar (Sorghum vulgare), these people consuming very little of milk or other foods of animal origin. Studies by Gopalan and others have shown that amino acid imbalance caused by an excess of leucine is the cause of pellagra in both jowar and maize eaters. Excess of leucine appears to interfere in the conversion of tryptophan to niacin.

Prevention

Pellagra is a preventable disease. A good mixed diet containing milk and/or meat 'is universally regarded as an essential part of prevention and treatment. Avoidance of total dependence on maize or sorghum is an important preventive measure. Pellagra is a disease of poverty. Given modern knowledge and opportunities for economic, agricultural and social development, there is every reason to hope that this disease could be eliminated.

Requirement

The recommended daily allowance is 6.6 rog/1000 energy intake. For further details see Table 3.11.

VITAMIN B_6

Pyridoxine (vitamin B_6) exists in three forms: pyridoxine, pyridoxal and pyridoxamine. It plays an important role in the metabolism of amino acids, fats and carbohydrate. It is widely distributed in foods, *e.g.*, milk, liver, meat, egg yolk, fish, whole grain cereals, legumes and vegetables. Pyridoxine deficiency is associated with peripheral neuritis. Riboflavin deficiency impairs the optimal utilization of pyridoxine. INH, an anti-tuberculosis drug is a recognized antagonist, and patients receiving INH are often provided with a supplement of pyridoxine (10 mg/day).

The requirements of adults vary directly with protein intake. Adults may need 2 mg/day; during pregnancy and lactation, 2.5 mg/day. Balanced diets usually contain pyridoxine, therefore deficiency is rare.

PANTOTHENIC ACID

There is a long standing evidence for a relation between pantothenic acid and adrenal cortical function. Recent work indicates a more specific role for pantothenic acid in the biosynthesis of corticosteroids. Human blood normally contains 18 to 35 mg of pantothenic acid per 100 mi, mostly present in the cells as coenzyme A. The daily requirement is set at 10 mg. All foods contribute to dietary intake. About 3 mg are excreted daily in urine.

FOLIATE

The recommended name is foliate, alternative name is folacin and the usual pharmaceutical preparation is folic acid.

Folic acid occurs in food in two forms: free folates and bound folates. The total folates represent both the groups. In man, free folate is rapidly absorbed, primarily from the proximal part of small intestine. The availability of bound folate is uncertain. Folic acid plays a role in the synthesis of the nucleic acids (which constitute the chromosomes). It is also needed for the normal development of blood cells in the marrow.

Sources

The name comes from the Latin word folia means (leaf) but foods such as: liver, meat, dairy products, eggs, milk, fruits and cereals are as good dietary sources as leafy vegetables. Overcooking destroys much of folic acid and thus contributes to foliate deficiency in man. Foliate deficiency has been reported in babies given milk foods subjected to heat sterilization.

Deficiency

Foliate deficiency may occur simply from a poor diet. It is commonly found in pregnancy and lactation, where requirements are increased. It results in megaloblastic anaemia, glossitis, cheilosis and gastrointestinal disturbances such as:

diarrhoea, distension and flatulence. Severe foliate deficiency may cause infertility or even sterility. There is also evidence that the administration of folic acid antagonists (*e.g.*, alcohol, pyrimethamine, and cotrimoxazole) in early pregnancy may produce abortions or congenital malformations.

The laboratory diagnosis of folate deficiency is based on measurement of serum and red cell folate concentrations, usually by microbiological assay.

Requirement

Body stores of folate are not large, about 5-10 mg, and therefore folate deficiency can develop quickly. Folic acid requirements are greatest in conditions where there is rapid cell multiplication, such as: during growth in young children and during pregnancy. Folic acid supplementation during pregnancy has been found to increase the birth weight of infants and decrease the incidence of low birth weight babies. Intake values recommended by ICMR (1989) are given below:

	Per day
Healthy adults	100 mcg
Pregnancy	400 mcg
Lactation	150 mcg
Children	100 mcg

VITAMIN B_{12}

Vitamin B_{12} is complex organo-metallic compound with a cobalt atom. The preparation which is therapeutically used is cynocobalamine, which is relatively cheap. Vitamin B_{12} co-operates with folate in the synthesis of DNA, so deficiency of either leads to megaloblastosis. Vitamin B_{12} has a separate biochemical role, unrelated to folate, in synthesis of fatty acids in myelin. The physiological mechanism for its absorption requires intrinsic factor from the stomach, and the complex is absorbed only at a special site in the terminal ileum.

Sources

Good sources are: liver, kidney, meat, fish, eggs, milk and cheese Vitamin. B_{12} is not of vegetable origin. It is also synthesized by bacteria in colon. Unlike folic acid vitamin B_{12}

is relatively heat stable. Liver is the main storage site of vitamin B_{12}. About 2 mg are stored in liver, and another 2 mg elsewhere in the body. These stores are sufficient to tide over any deficiency for one to three years. Because of these reserves, deficiency of vitamin B_{12} appears to be rare. Unlike folic acid, vitamin B12 is relatively heat stable.

Deficiency

Vitamin B_{12} deficiency is associated with megaloblastic anemia, (pernicious anemia), demy limiting neurological lesions in the spinal cord and infertility (in animal species). Dietary deficiency of B_2 may arise in subjects who are strict vegetarians and eat normal products. At the present time, there is little evidence that vitamin B_{12} deficiency anaemia represents an important public health problem.

Requirement

Intake values recommended by ICMR 1981 are as below:

1.	Normal adults	1 mcg
2.	Pregnancy	1.5 mcg
3.	Lactation	1.5 mcg
4.	Infants and children	0.2 mcg

VITAMIN C

Vitamin C (ascorbic acid) is a water-soluble vitamin. It is the most sensitive of all vitamins to heat. Man, monkey and guinea pig are perhaps the only species known to require vitamin C in their diet.

Functions

Vitamin C has an important role to play in tissue oxidation. It is needed for the formation of collagen, which accounts for 25 per cent of total body protein. Collagen provides a supporting matrix for the blood vessels and connective tissue and for bones and cartilage. That explains why in vitamin C deficiency this support fails with the result that local hemorrhages occur and the bones fracture easily. Vitamin C, by reducing ferric iron to ferrous iron, facilitates the absorption of iron from vegetable foods. It inhibits nitrosamine formation by the intestinal mucosa.

Other claims such as: prevention of common cold and protection against infections are not substantiated.

Sources

The main dietary sources of vitamin C are fresh fruits and green leafy vegetables. Traces of vitamin C occur is fresh meat and fish but scarcely any in cereals. Germinating pulses contain good amounts. Roots and tubers Contain small amounts. Amla or the Indian gooseberry is one of the richest sources of vitamin C both in the fresh as well as in the dry condition. Guavas are another cheap but rich source of this vitamin. The dietary sources of vitamin C are given in Table 3.11.

Table 3.11: Dietary sources of vitamin C

Mg per 100 g			
Fruits		*Vegetable*	
Amla	600	Amaranth	99
Guava	212	Cabbage	124
Lime	63	Spinach	28
Orange	30	Brinjal	12
Tomato	24	Cauliflower	56
Germinated pulses		Potatoes	17
Bengal Gram	16	Radish	15

Source: 157

Deficiency

Deficiency of vitamin C results in scurvy, the signs of which are swollen and bleeding gums, subcutaneous bruising or bleeding into the skin or joints, delayed wound healing, anemia and weakness. Scurvy which was once an important deficiency disease is no longer a disease of world importance.

Requirements

The estimated requirement for vitamin C has recently been raised from 40 to 60 mg with much larger doses advocated by some. The normal body when fully saturated contains about 5g of vitamin C.

Minerals

Minerals are the inorganic, indestructible elements that aids physiological processes within the body, without minerals, vitamins could not be absorbed. Minerals are readily excreted and are usually not toxic.

More than 50 chemical elements are found in the human: body, which are required for growth, repair and regulation of vital body functions. These can be divided into three major groups:

(a) *Major Minerals:* These include calcium, phosphorus, sodium, potassium and magnesium.

(b) *Trace Elements:* These are elements required by the body in quantities of less than a few milligrams per day, *e.g.*, iron, iodine, fluorine, zinc, copper cobalt, chromium, manganese, molybdenum, selenium, nickel, tin, silicon and vanadium. Many more have been added to the list in the last few years.

(c) *Trace Contaminants with no known Function:* These include lead, mercury, barium, boron, and aluminium.

Only a few mineral elements (*e.g.*, calcium, phosphorus, sodium, iron, fluorine, iodine) are associated with clearly recognizable clinical situations in man. For none of the other elements do we know with any certainty their metabolic roles, and much less the clinical effects of dietary insufficiency. The bioavailability of minerals such as: iron and zinc may be low in a total vegetarian diet because of the presence of substances such as: phytic acid. Besides, large amounts of dietary fibre may interfere with proper absorption. Man is not likely to suffer from trace element deficiencies as long as he is omnivorous. Surveys have shown that mineral deficiencies are no greater among vegetarians than among non-vegetarians. In fact, man's need for trace elements has not yet been precisely determined. Trace elements should not be used as dietary supplements, since excessive amounts can have injurious effects.

Macro-minerals are those minerals that the body needs in fairly large amounts: sodium, calcium phosphorous, magnesium, potassium, sculpture, and chloride. Trace minerals include iron, zinc, manganese, copper, iodine, and serious problems may result if excesses or deficiencies occur.

Although minerals are necessary for body function, there are limits on the amounts we should consume. Americans tend to overuse or under-use certain minerals.

CALCIUM

Calcium is a major mineral element of the body. It constitutes 1.5-2 per cent of the body weight of an adult human. An average adult body contains about 1200g of calcium of which over 98 per cent is found in the bones. The amount of calcium in the blood is usually about 10 mg/dl. The developing foetus requires about 30g of calcium. There is a dynamic equilibrium between the calcium in the blood and that in the skeleton; this equilibrium is maintained by the interaction of vitamin D, parathyroid hormone, and probably calcitonin.

The issue of calcium consumption has gained national attention with the rising incidence of' osteoporosis among elderly women. Although calcium plays a vital role in building strong bones anti teeth, muscle, contraction, blood clotting, nerve impulse transmissions, regulating heartbeat, and fluid balance within cells.

Because calcium intake is so important throughout life for maintaining a strong bone structure, it is critical to consume the *minimum* required amounts each day. Over half of our calcium intake usually comes from milk, one of the highest sources of dietary calcium. New calcium-fortified orange juice provides a good way to get calcium if you are not a milk drinker.

Functions

Ionized calcium in the plasma has many vital functions including formation of bones and teeth, coagulation of blood, contraction of muscles, cardiac action, milk production, relay of electrical and chemical messages that arrive at a cell's surface membrane to the biochemical machinery within the ceil, keeping the membranes of cells intact and in the metabolism of enzymes and hormones. It also plays a crucial role in the transformation of light to electrical impulses in the retina. In short, the calcium ion controls many life processes ranging from muscle contraction to cell division.

Sources

Calcium is readily available from many sources. Many green, leafy vegetables are good sources of calcium, whereas broccoli, cauliflower, and many peas and beans offer goal suppers. Many nuts, particularly almonds, Brazil nuts: and hazelnuts, and seeds, such as: citrus fruits, figs, raisins, and dried apricots – have moderate amounts. Bones meal is not a recommended calcium source because of contamination.

By far the best natural sources are milk and milk products, (*e.g.*, cheese, curd, skimmed milk and butter milk), eggs and fish. A litre of cow's milk provides about 1200 mg of calcium, and human milk about 300 mg. Calcium occurs in milk as calcium casein which is readily assimilated by the body. The cheapest dietary sources are green leafy vegetables, cereals and millets. The limiting factor in the complete absorption of calcium from green leafy vegetables (*e.g.*, spinach, amaranth) is the presence of oxalic acid with which calcium forms an insoluble compound, calcium oxalate which interferes with the absorption of calcium. Most cereals are generous providers of calcium, and the millet 'ragi' is particularly rich in calcium. Rice is very deficient in calcium. The bioavailability of calcium from cereals is poor because of the presence of phytic acid which forms an insoluble compound with calcium, calcium phytate. An additional source of calcium is drinking water which may provide up to 200 mg/day. Some fruits (*e.g.*, Sitaphal) contain good amounts of calcium.

Absorption

Overall, about 20-30 per cent of dietary calcium is normally absorbed. Absorption of calcium is enhanced by vitamin D and decreased by the presence of phytates, oxalates and fatty acids in the diet. Calcium absorption is regulated to some extent by the body's needs.

Deficiency

No clear-cut disease due to calcium deficiency has ever been observed, even under conditions of low intake. It has been established that if the intake of vitamin D is adequate, the problems of rickets and osteomalacia do not arise even with low calcium intake. On the other hand, no deleterious effects have been observed in man as a result of prolonged intakes of large amounts of dietary calcium, neither have any benefits been demonstrated.

We also know that sunlight increases the manufacture of vitamin D in the body and is therefore like having an extra calcium. Stress, however, contributes to calcium depletion. It is generally best to take calcium throughout the day, consuming it with foods containing protein, vitamin D, and vitamin C for optimum absorption.

Requirements

A daily intake of 400 to 500 mg of calcium has been suggested for adults. The physiological requirements are higher in children, expectant and nursing mothers.

PHOSPHORUS

Phosphorus is essential for the formation of bones and teeth. It plays an important part in all metabolisms. An adult human body contains about 400-700g of phosphorus as phosphates, most of this ccurs in bones and teeth. Phosphorus is widely distributed in foodstuffs; its deficiency rarely occurs. A large part of phosphorus present in vegetable foods occurs in combination with phytin and is available to the body only to the extent of 40-60 per cent. Phosphorus requirements have not been specifically considered by FAO/WHO Committees, but other groups of experts have suggested that phosphorus intake should be at least equal to calcium intakes in most age groups, except in infancy where the ratio suggested is 1:1.5.

SODIUM

Sodium is found in all body fluids. The adult human body contains about 100g of sodium ion. Sodium occurs in many foods, and is also added to food during cooking in the form of sodium chloride. Sodium is lost from the body through urine and sweat; that which is passed out in urine is regulated by the kidney but that which is lost by sweating is not controlled. Depletion of sodium chloride causes muscular cramps. The requirement of sodium chloride depends upon climate, occupation and physical activity. Adult requirement is about 10 to 15g. People engaged in hard work will need more.

POTASSIUM

The adult human body contains about 250g of potassium. Potassium occurs widely in food stuffs, so there is little likelihood of its deficiency. The daily requirement of potassium has not been determined accurately.

MAGNESIUM

Magnesium is a constituent of bones, and is present in all body cells. Human adult body contains about 25g of magnesium of which about half is found in the skeleton. It appears that magnesium is essential for the normal metabolism of calcium and potassium. Magnesium deficiency may occur in chronic alcoholics, cirrhosis of liver, toxaemias of pregnancy, protein-energy malnutrition and malabsorption syndrome. The principal clinical features attributed to magnesium deficiency are irritability, tetany, hyperreflexia and occasionally hyporeflexia. Requirements are estimated to be about 200-300 mg/day for adults.

IRON

Iron is of great importance in human nutrition. The adult human body contains between 3-4g of iron, of which about 60-70 per cent is present in the blood (Hb iron) as circulating iron, and the rest (1 to 1.5g) as storage iron. Each gram of haemoglobin contains about 3.34 mg of iron.

Functions

Iron is necessary for many functions in the body including formation of haemoglobin, brain development and function, regulation of body temperature, muscle activity, and catecholamine metabolism. Lack of iron directly affects the immune system; it diminishes the number of T-cells and the production of antibodies. Besides haemoglobin, iron is a component of myoglobin, the cytochromes, catalase and certain enzyme systems. Iron is essential for binding oxygen to the blood cells. The central function of iron is 'oxygen transport' and cell respiration.

Sources

There are two forms of iron: *(i)* haem-iron; and *(ii)* non-haem iron. Haem iron is better absorbed than non-haem iron. Foods rich in haem-iron are liver, meat, poultry and fish. They are not only important sources of readily available iron but they also promote the absorption of non-haem iron in plant foods eaten at the same time . The iron content of milk is low in all mammalian species, trori content of breast milk averages less than 0.2 mg/dl, and it is well utilized. Foods containing non-haem iron are those of vegetable origin, *e.g.*, cereals, green leafy vegetables, legumes' nuts, oilseeds, jaggery and dried fruits. They are important sources of iron in the diets of a large majority of Indian people. The bioavailability of non-haem iron is poor owing to the presence of phylates, oxalates, carbonates, phosphates and dietary fibre which interfere with iron absorption. Other foods which inhibit iron absorption are milk, eggs and tea. The Indian diet which is predominantly vegetarian contains large amounts of these inhibitors, *e.g.*, phytates in. bran, phosphates in egg yolk, tannin in tea and oxalates in vegetables. In some areas, significant amounts of iron may be derived from cooking in iron vessels.

Absorptions

Iron is mostly absorbed from duodenum and upper small intestine in the ferrous state, according to body needs. The rate of iron absorption is influenced by a great many factors like iron reserves of the subjects, the presence of inhibitors (*e.g.*, phosphates), and promoters (*e.g.*, ascorbic acid and ascorbic acid-rich foods) of iron absorption, and disorders of duodenum and jejunum (*e.g.*, coeliac disease, tropical sprue). Iron absorption is greater when there is an increased demand for iron, as for example during pregnancy. Iron absorption from habitual Indian diets is less than 5 per cent, the bioavailability being poor.

The absorbed iron is transported as plasma ferritin and stored in liver, spleen, bone marrow and kidney. The characteristic feature of iron metabolism is conservation. When red cells are broken do, the liberated iron is reutilized in the formation of new red cells.

Iron Losses

The total daily iron loss of an adult is probably 1mg, and about 2mg in menstruating women. Major routes of iron loss are:

(a) *Haemorrhage,* that is, wherever blood is lost, iron is lost, the causes of which may be physiological (*e.g.*, menstruation, childbirth) or pathological (*e.g.*, hookworms, malaria, hemorrhoids, peptic ulicer.

(b) *Basal losses,* such as: exception through tine, sweat and bile, and desquamated: surface cells. The recent widespread use of IUDs in the family planning programme is an additional cause of iron loss. IUDs have been shown to increase the average monthly blood loss by between 35 and 146 per cent depending upon the type of the device. Hormonal Contraceptives, on the other hand, decrease menstrual blood loss by about 50 per cent.

Iron Requirement

How much iron do adults need? Females aged 19-50 need about 18 milligrams per day, and males aged 19-50 need about 10 milligrams.

Iron Deficiency

When iron deficiency occurs, body cells receive less oxygen, and carbon dioxide wastes are removed less efficiently. Three stages of iron deficiency have been described:

(i) Free stage characters by decreased storage of iron without any other detectable abnormalities.

(ii) An intermediate stage of 'latent iron deficiency', that is, iron stores are exhausted, but anemia has not occurred as yet. Its recognition depends upon measurement of serum ferritin levels. The percentage saturation of transferring falls from a normal value of 30 per cent to

less than 15 per cent. This stage is the most widely percentage in India.

(iii) The third stage is that of overt iron deficiency when there is a decrease in the concentration of circulating hemoglobin due to impaired haemoglobin synthesis.

As result, the iron-deficient person feels tired and run down. The end result of iron deficiency is nutritional anaemia which is not a disease entity, anaemia can also result from blood loss, cancers, ulcers and other conditions.. It is rather a syndrome caused by malnutrition in its widest sense. Besides anaemia, there may be other functional disturbances such as: impaired cell-mediated immunity, reduced resistance to infection, increased morbidity and mortality and diminished work performance.

Generally, women are more likely to develop iron-deficiency problems because they typically eat less than men and their diets contain less iron. Women having heavy menstrual flow may be at greater risk. To date, considerable research has linked iron to a host of problems.

Iron Requirements

Because of the recycling of iron, only a small amount of iron is needed by the body. In general, iron requirements are greater, when there is rapid expansion of tissue and red cell mass, safe example during pregnancy, childhood and adolescence the iron requirements are more.

Iron deficiency may tax the immune system, causing it to function less effectively. Research suggesting a link between cardiovascular disease and elevated iron stores is inconclusive. Likewise, there appears to be a slight association between iron deficiency and cancer, but the mechanism remains inconclusive.

Iron overload, or iron toxicity due to ingesting too many iron-containing supplements, remains the leading cause of accidental poisoning in small children in the United States. Symptoms of toxicity include nausea, vomiting, diarrhoea, rapid heartbeat, weak pulse, dizziness, shock, and confession premium is necessary for the regulation of blood body fluids, transmission of nerve impulses, heart activity, and certain metallic functions. However, we consume much more than we need.

It is estimated that the average adults who does not sweat profusely needs only SGO milligrams of sodium per day, yet the average American consumes 6,000 to 12,000 milligrams. The RDA Subcommittee recommends re-enacting sodium to no more than 2,400 milligrams per day; less is better.

Fibre

Fibre, often referred to as 'bulk' or 'roughage,' is the indigestible portion of pant foods that helps move foods through the digestive system and softens stools by absorbing water. Fibre also helps to control weight by creating a feeling of fullness without adding extra calories.

Although nutritionists have been very vocal inadvocating increased fibres intake, the average American consumes only about 12 grams of fibre a day, about half the recommended daily amount of 25 grams.

Insoluble fibre, which is found in bran, whole-grain bread and cereals, and most fruits and vegetables is associated with these gastro-htestinal benefits and has also been found to reduce the risk for several forms of cancer. Soluble fibre appears to be a factor in lowering blood cholesterol levels, thereby reducing risk for cardiovascular disease. Major sources of soluble fibres in the diet include oat bran, dried beans, and some fruits and vegetables.

The best way to increase intake of dietary fibre is to eat more complex carbohydrates, such as: whole grains, fruits, vegetables, dried peas and bean, nuts, and seeds. As with most nutritional advice, however, too much of a good thing can pose problems.

Sudden increase in dietary fibre, may cause flatulence, cramping, or a bloated feeling. Consuming plenty of water or other liquids may reduce suck side effects.

A few years ago, fibre was thought by some to be the remedy for just about everything. Much of this hope was exaggerated. However, current research close support many benefits of fibre, such as: the following:

(i) *Protection against Colon and Rectal Cancer:* On of the leaching cause of cancer deaths in the United States, cancer is much rarer in countries having diets high in fibre and low in animal fat Several studies have supported the theory that fibre-rich diets, particularly those including insoluble fibre, prevents the development of precancerous growths.

Whether this is because consuming more fibre helps to move foods through the colon faster, thereby reducing the colons contact time with cancer-causing substances, because insoluble fibre reduces bile acids and certain bacterial enzymes that may promote, cancer, has remained in question. Research into the effects of fibre in colon cancer prevention continues.

(ii) *Protection against Heart Disease: Many* studieshave indicated that soluble fibre helps reduce blood cholesterol, Primarily by lowering LD L cholesterol. Whether this reduction is a direct effect or occurs instead through the displacement of fat calories by fibre calories or through intake of other-nutrients, such as: iron, remains in question.

(iii) *Protection against Obesity: Because* most high-fibre foods are high in carbohydrates and low in fat, they help control caloric intake. Many take longer to chew, which slows you down at the table makes you feel full sooner.

(iv) *Protection against Constipation:* Insoluble fibre, consumed, with adequate fluids, is the safest, most effective way to prevent or treat consumption. The fibre acts like a sponge, barbing moisture and producing softer, bulkier stools that are easily passed. Fibre also helps produce gas, which ha turn may initiate a bowel movement.

(v) *Protection against Diverticulitis: About* one American in ten over the age of 40 and at least one in three over 50 suffers-from diverticulitis, a condition in which tiny bulges or pouches farm on the large intestinal wall.

These bulges become irritated and cause chronic pain if under strain from constipation. Insoluble fibre helps to reduces constipation and discomfort.

(*vi*) *Protection against Diabetes:* Some studies have suggested that soluble fibre improves control of blood sugar and can reduce the need for insulin or medication in people with diabetes. Exactly; why is not clear, but soluble fibre seems to delay the emptying of the stomach and slow the absorption of glucose by the intestine.

Most experts behave that American should double their current consumption of dietary fibre-to 20 to-30 grams per day for most people and perhaps to 40 to 50s grams for others. There are some tips for increasing your fibre intake:

(*i*) Eat the skins of fruits and vegetables.

(*ii*) Spread out your fibre intake.

(*iii*) Drink plenty of liquids – at 1east 64 ounces of water daily.

(*iv*) Eat a variety of foods. Aim for at least five serving fruits and vegetables and three to six servings of whole-grain breads, cereals, and legumes per day throughout the day.

(*v*) Consume less processed food.

(*vi*) Get your fibres from feeds rather than pills or powders. Pills and powders do not supply enough essential nutrients.

Water: A Crucial Nutrient

If you were to go on a survival trip, which would you take with you – food or water? You may be surprised to learn that you could survive for much longer without food than you could without water.

Even in severe conditions, the averages Person can go for weeks without certain vitamins and minerals before expending serious deficiency symptoms. Dehydration, however, can cause serious problems within a matter of hours; after a few days without water, death is likely.

Just what function does water serve in the body? Between 50 and 60 per cent of our total body weight is water. The water in ours system bathes cells, aids in fluid and electrolyte balance, maintains PH balances, and transports molecules and cells throughout the body. Water is the major component of the blood, which carries oxygen and nutrients to the tissues and is responsible for maintaining cells in working orders.

How much water do you need? Most experts believe that six to eight glasses of water per day are necessary. Because of high concentrations of water in most of the foods we consume, however, the actual number of glasses needed each day is somewhat less than this.

Individual needs vary drastically according to dietary factors, age, size, environmental temperature and humidity levels, exercise, and the effectiveness of the individuals system. Certain diseases, such as: diabetes and cystic fibrosis, cause people to lose fluids at a rate necessitating a higher volume of fluid intake.

4

Different System of Human Body

WHAT IS A HUMAN BODY SYSTEM?

A system of human body means a collective functional unit made by several organs in which the organs work in complete co-ordination with one another. Organs cannot work alone because there are certain needs of every organ that need to be fulfilled and the organ itself cannot fulfill those needs. So all organs of human body need the support of other organs to perform their functions and in this way an organ system is formed.

Systems of the Human Body

Human body is made of ten different systems. All the systems require support and co-ordination of other systems to form a living and healthy human body. If any one of these systems is damaged, human body will become unstable and this lack of stability will ultimately lead to death. The instability caused by damage of one system cannot be stabilized by other systems because functions of one system cannot be performed by other systems. Knowledge of human body systems is very important for a medical professional because it is the base of all medical sciences and clinical practices. Although, generally, the structural aspects of human body systems are studied in anatomy and the functional aspects are studied in physiology but it is very important to have a co-ordination between the two subjects because knowledge of structure is incomplete without the knowledge of function and the knowledge of function is incomplete without the knowledge of structure.

A brief introduction to all the systems of human body is given in the Table 4.1 below:

Table 4.1:

Name	Components	Role
Skeletal system	Bones, Associated cartilages, Joints	Strength, Support, Shape, Protection, Leverage, Cell Production.
Muscular system	Muscles (Skeletal Muscles, Smooth Mucles, Cardiac Muscles)	Motor power for movements of body parts.
Nervous system	Brain, Spinal Cord, Nerves, Nerve Endings	Control and Co-ordination of all body functions (Nervous co-ordination).
Respiratory system	Lungs, Nose, Trachea, Bronchi, Bronchioles, Alveolar Sacs, Alveoli	Gaseou exchange.
Cardiovascular system	Heart, Blood vessels (Arteries, Veins and Capillaries), Blood	Flow of blood (and nutrients) through -out body.
Lymphatic system	Lymph vessels, Central lymphoid Tissue, Peripheral Lymphoid Organs, Lymphocytes	Drainage and Protection.
Endocrine system	Endocrine glands (Pituitary gland, Thyroid gland, Parathyroid glands, Adrenal glands, Pancreas (endocrine part), Testes (endocrine part), Ovary (endocrine part), Liver (endocrine part))	Regulation of body functions (Chemical co-ordination).

Contd...

Name	Components	Role
Digestive system	Alimentary Canal (Oral Cavity, Esophagus, Stomach, Small Intestine, Large Intestine, Anus), Liver, Pancreas, Salivary glands, Teeth, Tongue	Digestion and absorption of food.
Urinary system	Kidneys, Ureters, Urinary bladder, Urethra	Regulation of body's internal environment, and production and excretion of urine.
Male Reproductive system	Penis, Testes	Formation of sperms and semen, and fertilizing the female.
Female Reproductive system	Uterus, Ovaries, Vulva, Labia, Clitoris	Formation of eggs and bearing the fetus during development.

As you have observe in the above Table 4.1 that there are so many systems in our body but in this chapter you have learnt about only three systems of human body *i.e.,* digestive system, excretory system and respiratory system in detail.

Digestive System

The human digestive system is a complex series of organs and glands that processes food. In order to use the food we eat, our body has to break the food down into smaller molecules that it can process; it also has to excrete waste.

Most of the digestive organs (like the stomach and intestines) are tube like and contain the food as it makes its way through the body. The digestive system is essentially a long, twisting tube that runs from the mouth to the anus, plus a few other organs (like the liver and pancreas) that produce or store digestive chemicals.

The liver and pancreas are not a part of the digestive tract but they secrete certain juices or sections which do play a role in the process of digestion and absorption of food.

The whole process of digestion is accomplished in the time food remains in the digestive tract. The process of digestion starts from the ingestion or intake of food in the mouth. From here food passes to the other parts of the digestive tract. Each of these parts of the digestive tract (except the oesophagus, rectum and anus) contain some kind' of digestive juice. These juices are either secreted by that particular part of the tract or poured in from the other organs or glands of the body such as: liver and pancreas. These digestive juices contain chemical substances known as enzymes. Enzymes are proteins which help chemical reactions to proceed faster. They bring about changes in food substances without themselves undergoing any change.

DIGESTION OF FOOD

Let us now have a look at the overall process of digestion. Digestion takes place step-by-step at various sites in the digestive tract.

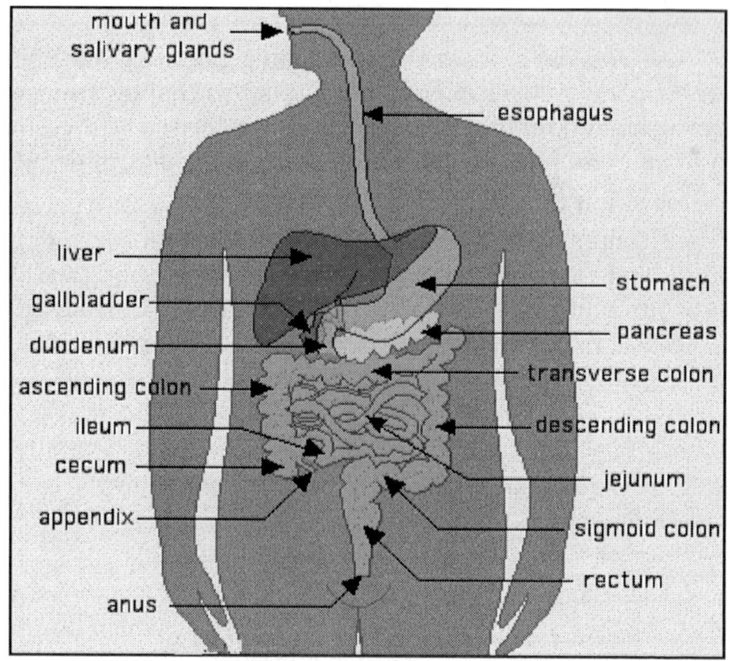

Digestive System

Mouth

As you have already noticed, the process of digestion begins in the mouth where food is chewed by the teeth and mixed with saliva, while the food is still in the mouth, it is acted upon by an enzyme which acts only on cooked carbohydrates find partially digests them or breaks them up into smaller units.

Throat

Also called the pharynx, the throat is the next destination for food you've eaten. From here, food travels to the esophagus or swallowing tube.

Esophagus

The esophagus is a muscular tube extending from the pharynx to the stomach. By means of a series of contractions, called peristalsis, the esophagus delivers food to the stomach. Just before the connection to the stomach there is a 'zone of high pressure,' called the lower esophageal sphincter; this is a 'valve' meant to keep food from passing backwards into the esophagus.

Stomach

The stomach is a large, sack like organ that churns the food and bathes it in a very strong acid (gastric acid). Food in the stomach that is partly digested and mixed with stomach acids is called chime. The chewed food mixed with Saliva then passes into the stomach.

Through the tube like structure called the oesophagus. Here it gets mixed with the digestive juice present in the stomach called gastric juice. Besides enzymes and water, gastric juice also contains small amounts of an acid called hydrochloric acid which makes it acidic in nature. Mixing of food with the gastric juice converts the food into a thin soup-like consistency. Gastric juice contains an enzyme which acts on proteins and brings about their partial digestion. Other nutrients in food remain chemically unchanged.

Small Intestine

The next stop in the digestive tract is the small intestine. The partially digested mass of food passes from the stomach into the small intestine. The small intestine not only contains intestinal juice (which is secreted from the small intestine itself) but also Secretions from the fiver and pancreas. The secretion from the liver is called bile and from the pancreas is knows as pancreatic juice. Bile aids in the digestion and absorption of fats (you will learn about the role of bile in fat digestion in Unit 3). Both pancreatic and intestinal juices contain enzymes which break down fats, proteins and carbohydrates into simpler substances. These simple substances ultimately reach the bloodstream.

Three organs play a pivotal role in helping the stomach and small intestine digest food:

(i) *Pancreas:* Among other functions, the oblong pancreas secretes enzymes into the small intestine. These enzymes break down protein, fat, and carbohydrates from the food we eat.

(ii) *Liver:* The liver has many functions, but two of its main functions within the digestive system are to make and secrete bile, and to cleanse and purify the blood coming from the small intestine containing the nutrients just absorbed.

(iii) *Gallbladder:* The gallbladder is a pear-shaped reservoir that sits just under the liver and stores bile. Bile is made in the liver then travels to the gallbladder through a channel called the cystic duct. During a meal, the gallbladder contracts, sending bile to the small intestine.

Once the nutrients have been absorbed and the leftover liquid has passed through the small intestine, what is left of the food you ate is handed over to the large intestine, or colon.

Large Intestine (Colon)

The colon is a 5 to 6 foot long muscular tube that connects the cecum (the first part of the large intestine to the rectum (the last part of the large intestine). It is made up of the cecum, the ascending (right) colon, the transverse (across) colon, the descending (left) colon, and the sigmoid colon (so-called for its "S" shape; the Greek letter for S is called the sigma), which connects to the rectum.

Stool, or waste left over from the digestive process, is passed through the colon by means of peristalsis (contractions), first in a liquid state and ultimately in solid form as the water is removed from the stool. A stool is stored in the sigmoid colon until a 'mass movement' empties it into the rectum once or twice a day. It normally takes about 36 hours for stool to get through the colon. The stool itself is mostly food debris and bacteria. These bacteria perform several useful functions, such as: synthesizing various vitamins, processing waste products and food particles, and protecting against harmful bacteria. When the descending colon becomes full of stool, or feces, it empties its contents into the rectum to begin the process of elimination.

Rectum

The rectum (Latin for 'straight') is an 8 inch chamber that connects the colon to the anus. It is the rectum's job to receive stool from the colon, to let you know there is stool to be evacuated, and to hold the stool until evacuation happens. When anything (gas or stool) comes into the rectum, sensors send a message to the brain. The brain then decides if the rectal contents can be released or not, if they can, the sphincters (muscles) relax and the rectum contracts, expelling its contents. If the contents cannot be expelled, the sphincters contract and the rectum accommodates, so that the sensation temporarily goes away.

Anus

The anus is the last part of the digestive tract. It consists of the pelvic floor muscles and the two anal sphincters (internal and external muscles). The lining of the upper anus is specialized to detect rectal contents. It lets us know whether the contents are liquid, gas, or solid. The pelvic floor muscle creates an angle between the rectum and the anus that stops stool from coming out when it is not supposed to. The anal sphincters provide fine control of stool. The internal sphincter keeps us from going to the bathroom when we are asleep, or otherwise unaware of the presence of stool. When we get an urge to go to the bathroom, we rely on our external sphincter to keep the stool in until we can get to the toilet.

ABSORPTION OF FOOD

Where is food absorbed? You would have realized by now that absorption takes place in the small intestine. The end products of digestion or the nutrients present in the small intestine can be used by the body only when they enter the bloodstream. This process of movement of digested food or nutrients across the intestinal wall to the bloodstream is termed absorption of food. The wall of the small intestine is made up of numerous folds or finger like projections known as with. The presence of these tremendously increase the total area from which action can take place. Most of the nutrients are absorbed from the upper part of the small intestine though some are absorbed.

UTILIZATION OF FOOD

How is food utilized? In order to be utilized for specific functions the absorbed end products or the nutrients from the food we eat further undergo chemical changes. They are either further broken down to release energy or are used to form more complex substances. These substances can then be used to manufacture more complex substances or can be stored in the body. We use certain terms to refer to these processes. Let us learn these terms.

Metabolism is a general term. It is just a small word referring to all the chemical changes that take place in the cells after the end products of digestion are absorbed. It is of two types – *(i)* break down of complex substances into simpler ones; and *(ii)* manufacture of complex substances from simple ones. We have two terms referring to each of these processes. Let us learn these.

Anabolism is the term used to refer to all the chemical reactions, which simple substances are used to manufacture more complicated ones and catabolism includes all the chemical reactions by which complex substances are further broken down to simpler components.

Excretory System

The excretory system is the system of an organism's body that performs the function of excretion, the bodily process of discharging wastes.

The Excretory system is responsible for the elimination of wastes produced by homeostasis.

There are several parts of the body that are involved in this process, such as: sweat glands, the liver, the lungs and the kidney system.

Every human has two kidneys. Each kidney is made up of three sections: *(i)* the renal cortex; *(ii)* the renal medulla; and *(iii)* the renal pelvis.

The blood arrives at the kidney via the renal artery, which splits into many afferent arterioles. These arterioles go to the Bowman's Capsules of nephrons, where the wastes are taken out of the blood by pressure filtration.

Peritubular capillaries also surround the nephron so substances can be taken in and out of the blood.

The renal cortex is the outer layer of the kidney and the medulla is the inner layer of the kidney.

The renal pelvis takes urine away from the kidney via the ureter.

Both of the ureters lead the urine into the body's only urinary bladder, which expands and sends nerve impulses when full.

From there, urine is expelled through the urethra and out of the body.

The Human Excretory System

The urinary system is made-up of the kidneys, ureters, bladder, and urethra. The nephron, an evolutionary modification of the nephridium, is the kidney's functional unit. Waste is filtered from the blood and collected as urine in each kidney. Urine leaves the kidneys by ureters, and collects in the bladder. The bladder can distend to store urine that eventually leaves through the urethra.

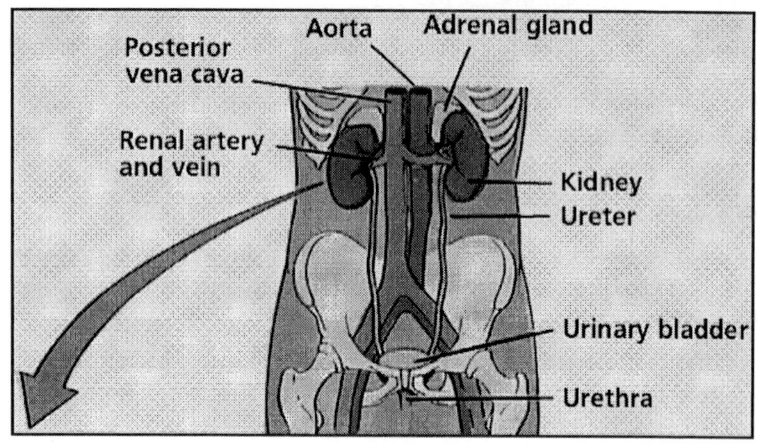

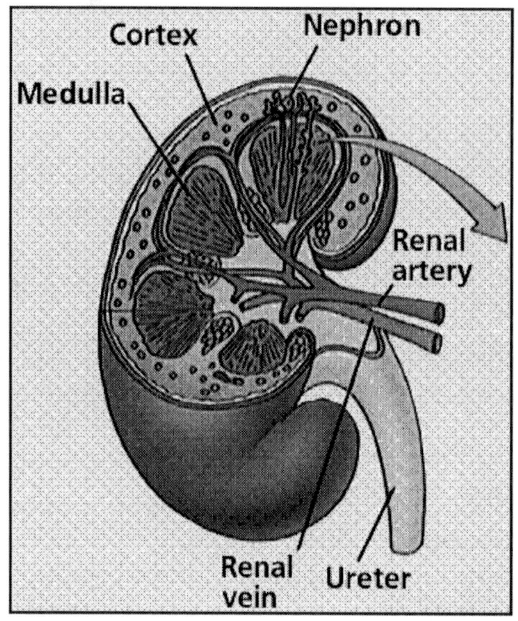

The Nephron

The nephron consists of a cup-shaped capsule containing capillaries and the glomerulus, and a long renal tube. Blood flows into the kidney through the renal artery, which branches into capillaries associated with the glomerulus. Arterial

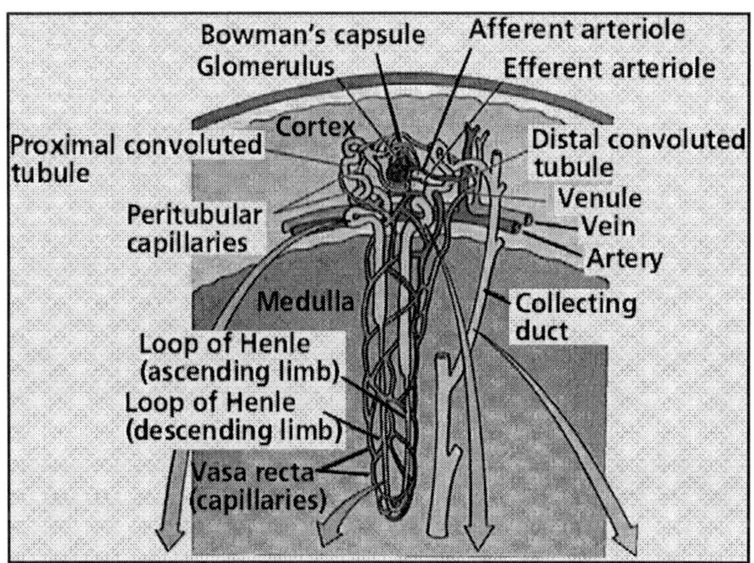
Bowman's capsule
Glomerulus
Afferent arteriole
Efferent arteriole
Cortex
Proximal convoluted tubule
Distal convoluted tubule
Venule
Vein
Artery
Peritubular capillaries
Medulla
Collecting duct
Loop of Henle (ascending limb)
Loop of Henle (descending limb)
Vasa recta (capillaries)

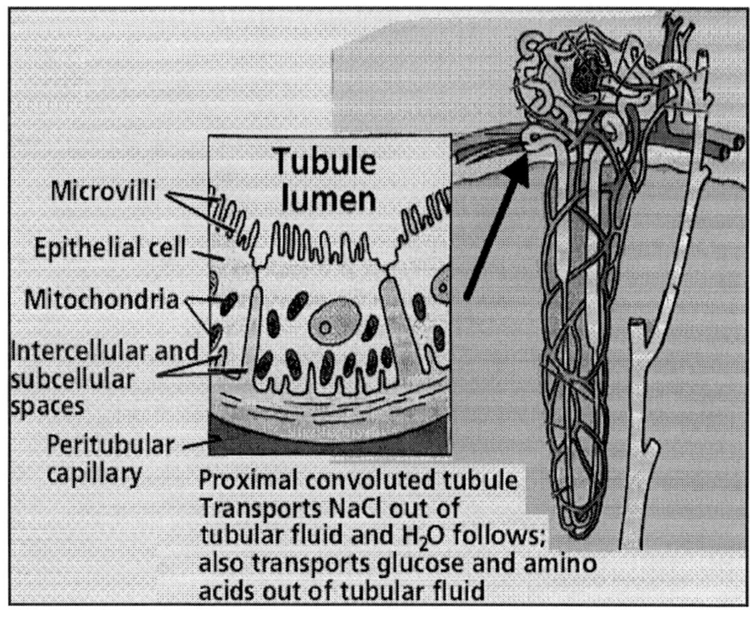
Tubule lumen
Microvilli
Epithelial cell
Mitochondria
Intercellular and subcellular spaces
Peritubular capillary
Proximal convoluted tubule
Transports NaCl out of tubular fluid and H_2O follows; also transports glucose and amino acids out of tubular fluid

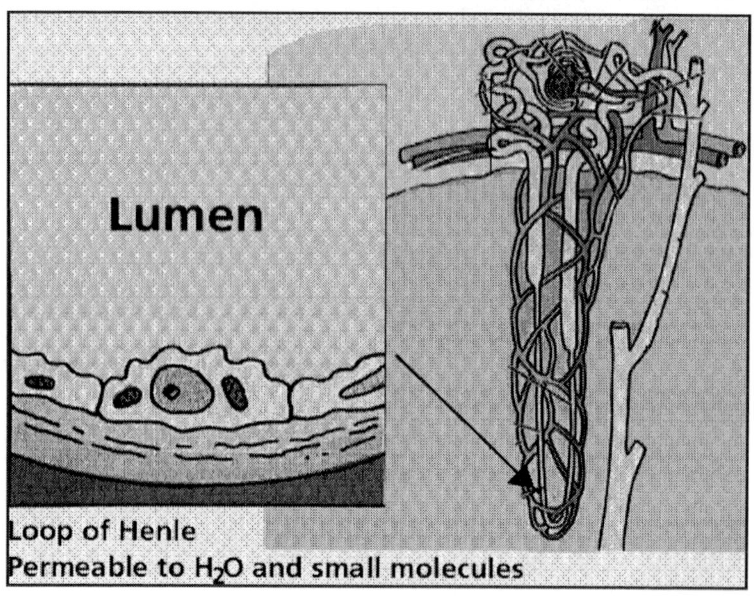

Loop of Henle
Permeable to H_2O and small molecules

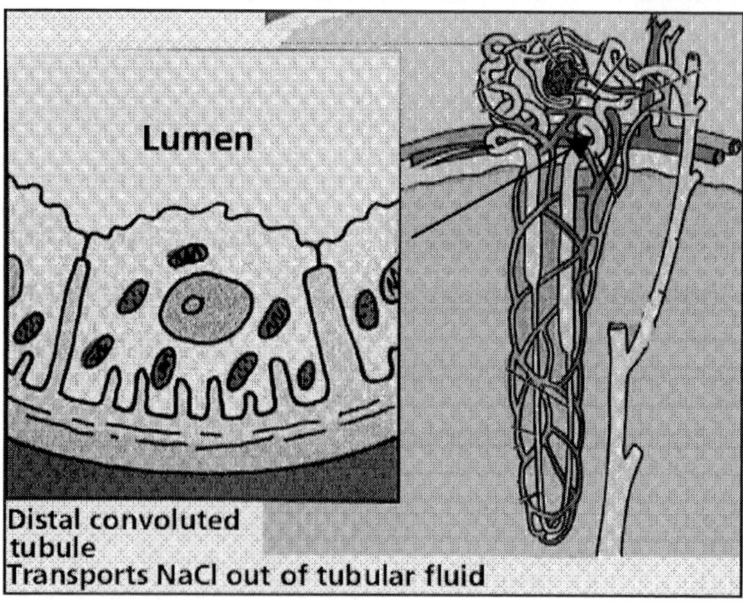

Distal convoluted tubule
Transports NaCl out of tubular fluid

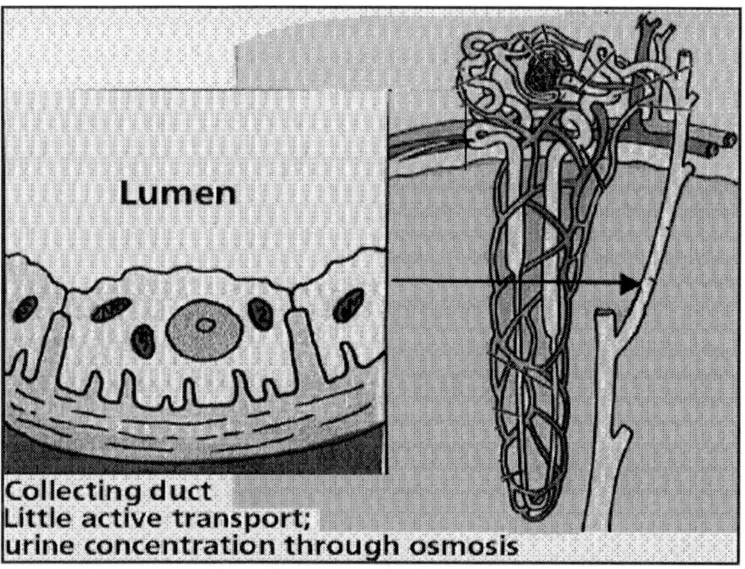

Human Excretory System and the Details of the Kidney

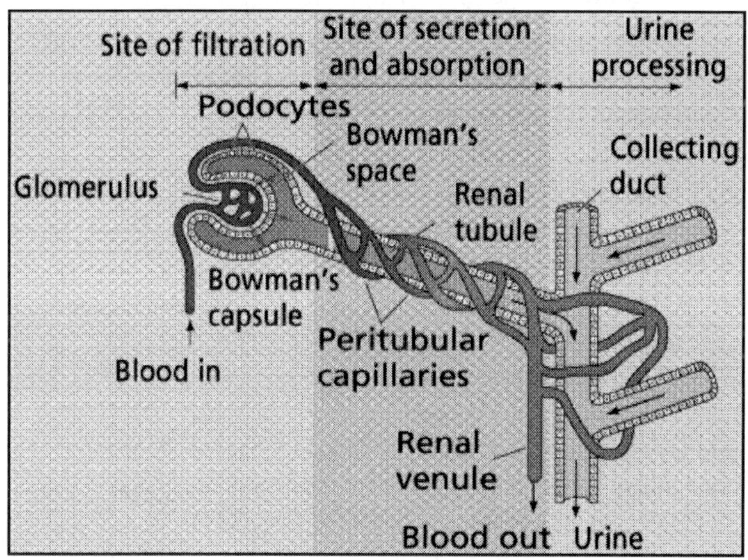

Filtration of the Blood in the Fine Structure of the Kidneys

pressure causes water and solutes from the blood to filter into the capsule. Fluid flows through the proximal tubule, which include the loop of Henle, and then into the distal tubule. The distal tubule empties into a collecting duct. Fluids and solutes are returned to the capillaries that surround the nephron tubule.

The nephron has three functions:

1. Glomerular filtration of water and solutes from the blood.
2. Tubular reabsorption of water and conserved molecules back into the blood.
3. Tubular secretion of ions and other waste products from surrounding capillaries into the distal tubule.

Nephrons filter 125 ml of body fluid per minute; filtering the entire body fluid component 16 times each day. In a 24 hour period nephrons produce 180 liters of filtrate, of which 178.5 liters are reabsorbed. The remaining 1.5 liters forms urine.

Urine Production

1. Filtration in the glomerulus and nephron capsule.
2. Reabsorption in the proximal tubule.
3. Tubular secretion in the Loop of Henle.

Components of the Nephron

- *Glomerulus*: mechanically filters blood.
- *Bowman's Capsule*: mechanically filters blood.
- *Proximal Convoluted Tubule*: Reabsorbs 75 per cent of the water, salts, glucose, and amino acids.
- *Loop of Henle*: Countercurrent exchange, which maintains the concentration gradient.
- *Distal Convoluted Tubule*: Tubular secretion of H ions, potassium, and certain drugs.

Kidney Stones

In some cases, excess wastes crystallize as kidney stones. They grow and can become a painful irritant that may require surgery or ultrasound treatments. Some stones are small enough to be forced into the urethra, others are the size of huge, massive boulders (or so I am told).

Kidney Function

Kidneys perform a number of homeostatic functions:

1. Maintain volume of extracellular fluid.
2. Maintain ionic balance in extracellular fluid.
3. Maintain pH and osmotic concentration of the extracellular fluid.
4. Excrete toxic metabolic by-products such as: urea, ammonia, and uric acid.

Hormone Control of Water and Salt

Water reabsorption is controlled by the antidiuretic hormone (ADH) in negative feedback. ADH is released from the pituitary gland in the brain. Dropping levels of fluid in the blood signal the hypothalamus to cause the pituitary to release ADH into the blood. ADH acts to increase water absorption in the kidneys. This puts more water back in the blood, increasing the concentration of the urine. When too much fluid is present in the blood, sensors in the heart signal the hypothalamus to cause a reduction of the amounts of ADH in the blood. This increases the amount of water absorbed by the kidneys, producing large quantities of a more dilute urine.

Aldosterone, a hormone secreted by the kidneys, regulates the transfer of sodium from the nephron to the blood. When sodium levels in the blood fall, aldosterone is released into the blood, causing more sodium to pass from the nephron to the blood. This causes water to flow into the blood by osmosis. Renin is released into the blood to control aldosterone.

Disruption of Kidney Function

Infection, environmental toxins such as: mercury, and genetic disease can have devastating results by causing disruption of kidney function. Many kidney problems can be treated by dialysis, where a machine acts as a kidney. Kidney transplants are an alternative to dialysis.

Respiratory System

What is the Respiratory System

Your respiratory system is made up of the organs in your body that help you to breathe. Remember, that Respiration =

Breathing. The goal of breathing is to deliver oxygen to the body and to take away carbon dioxide.

Parts of the Respiratory System

The cells of the human body require a constant stream of oxygen to stay alive. The respiratory system provides oxygen to the body's cells while removing carbon dioxide, a waste product that can be lethal if allowed to accumulate. There are three major parts of the respiratory system: *(i)* the airway; *(ii)* the lungs; and *(ii)* the muscles of respiration. The airway, which includes: the nose, mouth, pharynx, larynx, trachea, bronchi, and bronchioles, carries air between the lungs and the body's exterior.

Anatomy of the Respiratory System

Nose and Nasal Cavity

The nose and nasal cavity form the main external opening for the respiratory system and are the first section of the body's airway – the respiratory tract through which air moves. The nose is a structure of the face made of cartilage, bone, muscle, and skin that supports and protects the anterior portion of the nasal cavity. The nasal cavity is a hollow space within the nose and skull that is lined with hairs and mucus membrane. The function of the nasal cavity is to warm, moisturize, and filter air entering the body before it reaches the lungs. Hairs and mucus lining the nasal cavity help to trap dust, mold, pollen and other environmental contaminants before they can reach the inner portions of the body. Air exiting the body through the nose returns moisture and heat to the nasal cavity before being exhaled into the environment.

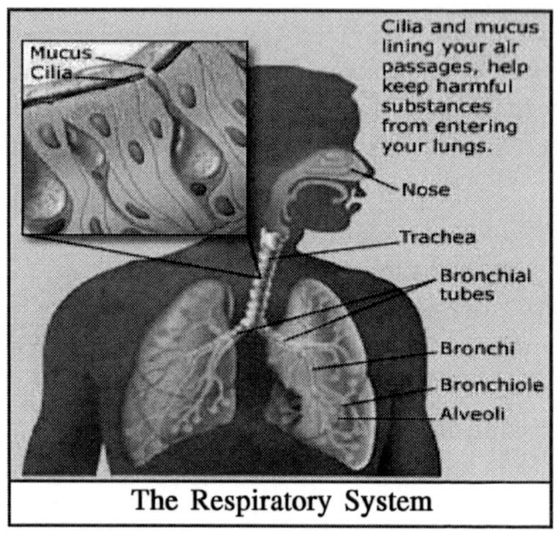

The Respiratory System

Mouth

The mouth, also known as the oral cavity, is the secondary external opening for the respiratory tract. Most normal breathing takes place through the nasal cavity, but the oral cavity can be used to supplement or replace the nasal cavity's functions when needed. Because the pathway of air entering the body from the mouth is shorter than the pathway for air entering from the nose, the mouth does not warm and moisturize the air entering the lungs as well as the nose performs this function. The mouth also lacks the hairs and sticky mucus that filter air passing through the nasal cavity. The one advantage of breathing through the mouth is that its shorter distance and larger diameter allows more air to quickly enter the body.

Pharynx

The pharynx, also known as the throat, is a muscular funnel that extends from the posterior end of the nasal cavity to the superior end of the esophagusand larynx. The pharynx is divided into three regions: *(i)* the nasopharynx; *(ii)* oropharynx; and *(iii)* laryngopharynx. The nasopharynx is the superior region of the pharynx found in the posterior of the nasal cavity. Inhaled air from the nasal cavity passes into the nasopharynx and descends through the oropharynx, located in the posterior of the oral cavity. Air inhaled through the oral cavity enters the pharynx at the oropharynx. The inhaled air then descends into the laryngopharynx where it is diverted into the opening of the larynx by the epiglottis. The epiglottisis a flap of elastic cartilage that acts as a switch between the trachea and the esophagus. Because the pharynx is also used to swallow food, the epiglottis ensures that air passes into the trachea by covering the opening to the esophagus. During the process of swallowing, the epiglottis moves to cover the trachea to ensure that food enters the esophagus and to prevent choking.

Larynx

The larynx, also known as the voice box, is a short section of the airway that connects the laryngopharynx and the trachea. The larynx is located in the anterior portion of the neck, just inferior to the hyoid bone and superior to the trachea. Several cartilage structures make up the larynx and give it its structure. The epiglottis is one of the cartilage pieces of the larynx and serves as the cover of the larynx during swallowing. Inferior to the epiglottis is the thyroid cartilage, which is often referred to as the Adam's apple as it is most commonly enlarged and visible in adult males. The thyroid holds open the anterior end of the larynx and protects the vocal folds. Inferior to the thyroid cartilage is the ring-shaped cricoid cartilage which holds the larynx open and supports its posterior end. In addition to cartilage, the larynx contains special structures known as vocal folds, which allow the body to produce the sounds of speech and singing. The vocal folds are folds of mucous membrane that vibrate to produce vocal sounds. The tension and vibration speed of the vocal folds can be changed to change the pitch that they produce.

Trachea

The trachea, or windpipe, is a 5 inch long tube made of C shaped hyaline cartilage rings lined with pseudostratified ciliated columnar epithelium. The trachea connects the larynx to the bronchi and allows air to pass through the neck and into the thorax. The rings of cartilage making up the trachea allow it to remain open to air at all times. The open end of the cartilage rings faces posteriorly toward the esophagus, allowing the esophagus to expand into the space occupied by the trachea to accommodate masses of food moving through the esophagus.

The main function of the trachea is to provide a clear airway for air to enter and exit the lungs. In addition, the epithelium lining the trachea produces mucus that traps dust and other contaminants and prevents it from reaching the lungs. Cilia on the surface of the epithelial cells move the mucus superiorly toward the pharynx where it can be swallowed and digested in the gastrointestinal tract.

Bronchi and Bronchioles

At the inferior end of the trachea, the airway splits into left and right branches known as the primary bronchi. The left and right bronchi run into each lung before branching off into smaller secondary bronchi. The secondary bronchi carry air into the lobes of the lungs – 2 in the left lung and 3 in the right lung. The secondary bronchi in turn split into many smaller tertiary bronchi within each lobe. The tertiary bronchi split into many smaller bronchioles that spread throughout the lungs. Each bronchiole further splits into many smaller branches less than a millimeter in diameter called terminal bronchioles. Finally, the millions of tiny terminal bronchioles conduct air to the alveoli of the lungs.

As the airway splits into the tree like: branches of the bronchi and bronchioles, the structure of the walls of the airway begins to change. The primary bronchi contain many C-shaped cartilage rings that firmly hold the airway open and give the bronchi a cross-sectional shape like a flattened circle or a letter D. As the bronchi branch into secondary and tertiary bronchi, the cartilage becomes more widely spaced and more smooth muscle and elastin protein is found in the walls. The bronchioles differ from the structure of the bronchi in that they do not contain any cartilage at all. The presence of smooth muscles and elastin allow the smaller bronchi and bronchioles to be more flexible and contractile.

The main function of the bronchi and bronchioles is to carry air from the trachea into the lungs. Smooth muscle tissue in their walls helps to regulate airflow into the lungs. When greater volumes of air are required by the body, such as: during exercise, the smooth muscle relaxes to dilate the bronchi and bronchioles. The dilated airway provides less resistance to airflow and allows more air to pass into and out of the lungs. The smooth muscle fibers are able to contract during rest to prevent hyperventilation. The bronchi and bronchioles also use the mucus and cilia of their epithelial lining to trap and move dust and other contaminants away from the lungs.

Lungs

The lungs are the main organs of the respiratory system. In the lungs oxygen is taken into the body and carbon dioxide

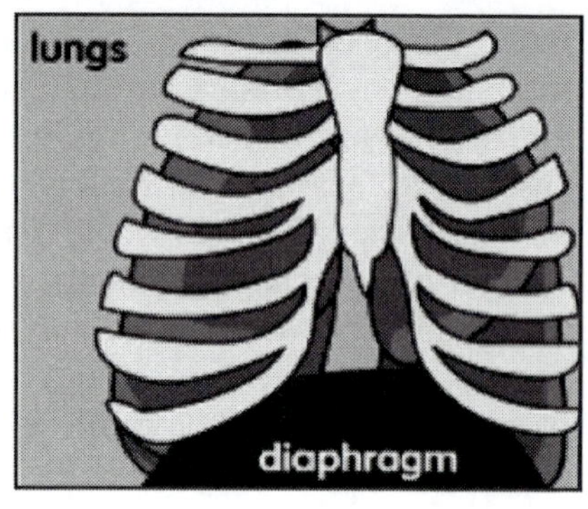

is breathed out. The red blood cells are responsible for picking up the oxygen in the lungs and carrying the oxygen to all the body cells that need it. The red blood cells drop off the oxygen to the body cells, then pick up the carbon dioxide which is a waste gas product produced by our cells. The red blood cells transport the carbon dioxide back to the lungs and we breathe it out when we exhale.

The lungs are a pair of large, spongy organs found in the thorax lateral to the heart and superior to the diaphragm. Each lung is surrounded by a pleural membrane that provides the lung with space to expand as well as a negative pressure space relative to the body's exterior. The negative pressure allows the lungs to passively fill with air as they relax. The left and right lungs are slightly different in size and shape due to the heart pointing to the left side of the body. The left lung is therefore slightly smaller than the right lung and is made up of 2 lobes while the right lung has 3 lobes.

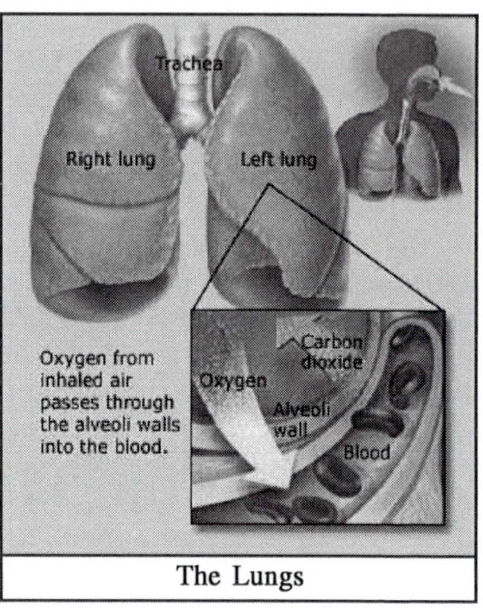

The Lungs

The interior of the lungs is made up of spongy tissues containing many capillaries and around 30 million tiny sacs known as alveoli. The alveoli are cup-shaped structures found at the end of the terminal bronchioles and surrounded by capillaries. The alveoli are lined with thin simple squamous epithelium that allows air entering the alveoli to exchange its gases with the blood passing through the capillaries.

Muscles of Respiration

Surrounding the lungs are sets of muscles that are able to cause air to be inhaled or exhaled from the lungs. The principal muscle of respiration in the human body is the diaphragm, a thin sheet of skeletal muscle that forms the floor of the thorax. When the diaphragm contracts, it moves inferiorly a few inches into the abdominal cavity, expanding the space within the thoracic cavity and pulling air into the lungs. Relaxation of the diaphragm allows air to flow back out the lungs during exhalation.

Between the ribs are many small intercostal muscles that assist the diaphragm with expanding and compressing the lungs. These muscles are divided into 2 groups: the internal intercostal muscles and the external intercostal muscles. The internal intercostal muscles are the deeper set of muscles and depress the ribs to compress the thoracic cavity and force air to be exhaled from the lungs. The external intercostal are found superficial to the internal intercostal and function to elevate the ribs, expanding the volume of the thoracic cavity and causing air to be inhaled into the lungs.

Physiology of the Respiratory System

Pulmonary Ventilation

Pulmonary ventilation is the process of moving air into and out of the lungs to facilitate gas exchange. The respiratory system uses both a negative pressure system and the contraction of muscles to achieve pulmonary ventilation. The negative pressure system of the respiratory system involves the establishment of a negative pressure gradient between the alveoli and the external atmosphere. The pleural membrane seals the lungs and maintains the lungs at a pressure slightly below that of the atmosphere when the lungs are at rest. This results in air following the pressure gradient and passively filling the lungs at rest. As the lungs fill with air, the pressure within the lungs rises until it matches the atmospheric pressure. At this point, more air can be inhaled by the contraction of the diaphragm and the external intercostal muscles, increasing the volume of the thorax and reducing the pressure of the lungs below that of the atmosphere again.

To exhale air, the diaphragm and external intercostal muscles relax while the internal intercostal muscles contract to reduce the volume of the thorax and increase the pressure within the thoracic cavity. The pressure gradient is now reversed, resulting in the exhalation of air until the pressures inside the lungs and outside of the body are equal. At this point, the elastic nature of the lungs causes them to recoil back to their resting volume, restoring the negative pressure gradient present during inhalation.

External Respiration

External respiration is the exchange of gases between the air filling the alveoli and the blood in the capillaries surrounding the walls of the alveoli. Air entering the lungs from the atmosphere has a higher partial pressure of oxygen and a lower partial pressure of carbon dioxide than does the blood in the capillaries. The difference in partial pressures causes the gases to diffuse passively along their pressure gradients from high to low pressure through the simple squamous epithelium lining of the alveoli. The net result of external respiration is the movement of oxygen from the air into the blood and the movement of carbon dioxide from the blood into the air. The oxygen can then be transported to the body's tissues while carbon dioxide is released into the atmosphere during exhalation.

Internal Respiration

Internal respiration is the exchange of gases between the blood in capillaries and the tissues of the body. Capillary blood has a higher partial pressure of oxygen and a lower partial pressure of carbon dioxide than the tissues through which it passes. The difference in partial pressures leads to the diffusion of gases along their pressure gradients from high to low pressure through the endothelium lining of the capillaries. The net result of internal respiration is the diffusion of oxygen into the tissues and the diffusion of carbon dioxide into the blood.

Transportation of Gases

The two major respiratory gases, *(i)* oxygen; and *(ii)* carbon dioxide, are transported through the body in the blood. Blood plasma has the ability to transport some dissolved oxygen and carbon dioxide, but most of the gases transported in the blood are bonded to transport molecules. Hemoglobin is an important transport molecule found in red blood cells that carries almost 99 per cent of the oxygen in the blood. Hemoglobin can also carry a small amount of carbon dioxide from the tissues back to the lungs. However, the vast majority of carbon dioxide is carried in the plasma as bicarbonate ion. When the partial pressure of carbon dioxide is high in the tissues, the enzyme carbonic anhydrase catalyzes a reaction between carbon dioxide and water to form carbonic acid. Carbonic acid then dissociates into hydrogen ion and bicarbonate ion. When the partial pressure of carbon dioxide is low in the lungs, the reactions reverse and carbon dioxide is liberated into the lungs to be exhaled.

Homeostatic Control of Respiration

Under normal resting conditions, the body maintains a quiet breathing rate and depth called eupnea. Eupnea is maintained until the body's demand for oxygen and production of carbon dioxide rises due to greater exertion. Autonomic chemoreceptors in the body monitor the partial pressures of oxygen and carbon dioxide in the blood and send signals to the respiratory center of the brain stem. The respiratory center then adjusts the rate and depth of breathing to return the blood to its normal levels of gas partial pressures.

5

Common Infectious Diseases

INTRODUCTION

You are aware that children are very prone to infections. The infections are mused by micro-organisms which are very minute and can be seen only through a micro-scope. Measles, tuberculosis, whooping cough are three such infectious diseases commonly found in children. What is the causative agent? How does it spread? How do we identify these diseases? What can we do to prevent our children from getting these diseases? This unit provides answer to these crucial questions.

In this chapter we will learn about the causes, complications, prevention control measures for each of the infectious diseases. Before we go in to detail you should be familiar with the following terms.

- *Infection:* The entry and development or multiplication of an infectious agent in the body of man or animals. Infection need not always mean infectious disease. The infection, sometimes, may be in apparent *i.e.,* without any recognisable clinical signs or symptoms. This is known as sub clinical infection.
- *Infectious Diseases:* A disease of man or animals resulting from an infection. The persons suffering an infectious disease exhibit clinical sign or symptoms from which one can diagnose the disease.

- *Infectious Agent:* An organism, chiefly a micro-organism that is capable of producing an infectious disease. Most of the infections are caused by bacteria or virus which cannot be seen by naked eye and require either simple or sophisticated microscope to see them.
- *Incubation Period*: The time interval between exposure to an infectious agent and appearance of the first sign or symptom of the disease in question.
- *Communicable Disease:* An illness, due to a specific infectious agent or its toxic products, which arises through transmission of agent or its products from a reservoir to a susceptible host, either directly, as from an infected person or animal, or directly, through an intermediate plant or animal host, vector or the inanimate environment.

MEASLES

Measles is a viral disease which generally attacks children, around one year of age. It is one of the important and common childhood infections. Measles is endemic in most of the countries of the world. In India, every year about 14 million children suffer from measles. It is estimated that 20,000 children die every year in our country due to complications from measles.

The Disease – What Causes it? Who gets it? How and When does it Spread?

What Causes Measles?

The disease is caused by the measles virus. Viruses you know are micro-organisms which can be seen only through sophisticated micro-scope.

Who gets the Disease?

- *Age:* The disease is common in childhood. Most of file children have an attack of measles by the time they complete the age of 3 years. In about a third of all cases with measles, it occurs under the age of one year.
- *Socio-economic Factors:* Measles is particularly severe amongst poor communities. Of many adverse influences of poor socio-economic status on child, poor nutrition,

both before and during the attack of measles, plays a major part in the severity and outcome of the infection. Epidemics tend to occur at 2 to 4 year intervals in crowded large cities, particularly in the urban slum areas. In conditions of poor environment, children get measles at an earlier age. In middle income families, it occurs later around the school age.

- *Sex:* Incidence of measles is equal among both the sexes.
- *Seasons:* The disease is more prevalent in winter.

How does it Spread

It is spread through droplets (either during coughing or sneezing) or direct contact with secretions from nose or throat or urine of persons infected with measles. It is one of the most readily transmissible of the communicable diseases. Articles recently contaminated with saliva or nasal discharges may also convey infection. An attack of measles in the cause of pregnant women may lead to abortion.

- *Incubation Period:* The disease takes, on an average, about 10 days varying from 8 to 13 days, to occur from the time of exposure to a patient with measles to the onset of fever. The skin rash appears about 14 days after exposure to an infected child.
- *Period of Communicability:* The disease is communicable from the beginning of onset of fever to 4-6 days after appearance of the skin rash. Measles is very infections and about 90 per cent of susceptible family members coming in contact with the patient (family contacts) acquire the disease. In other words, other children, who had not got measles earlier, in the household of the patient are likely to catch the disease.
- *Susceptibility:* Practically all persons are susceptible. After an attack, a person usually acquires permanent immunity. In other words, an individual suffers from measles only once in life time. Infants born of mothers who have had the disease are ordinarily immune (*i.e.,* do not develop the disease) for approximately the first 6 months of life.

Symptoms and Complications

Measles is an acute (short and sudden onset) communicable disease. It starts as mild fever, cough and running nose. There will be conjunctivitis (reddening of the eyes). If you examine the inside of mouth, you can find characteristic greyish white spots on a red base on the mucous membrane of the mouth (a membrane, secreting mucus, lining the mouth). A day or two later typical skin rash (eruptions on the skin) which is dusky red in colour appears *i.e.,* third to seventh day alter the onset of fever. The rash appears first on the face and spreads to the body and generally lasts for 4-5 days. Measles is rather severe among children who are malnourished.

Complications of Measles

Measles is an important public health problem because it leaves the children in a debilitated condition (very weak). Common complication after an attack of measles is severe respiratory infection leading to broncho-pneumonia (infection of the lungs) which may end in death. One of the commonest complications is severe diarrhoea which quite often leads m malnutrition. Measles and nutritional status of the child are very closely associated. If you carefully question the mothers of the children suffering from severe forms of malnutrition, always, they would tell you that the children Middle ear infection, mental retardation can also occur as complications after an attack of measles. Measles is known to contribute to the damage of the cornea (black portion of the eye) leading to blindness. Measles also aggravates Vitamin A deficiency in children and leads to blindness.

Prevention and Management

Prevention control measures for measles are discussed below:

- *Prevention of Measles through Vaccination:* Vaccination is the simplest and best method to prevent measles. Normally all children at 12 months of age or as soon there after as possible are given measles immunisation. A single injection protects 95 per cent of susceptible children from the disease for over 12 years and probably for life. After vaccination majority have minimal infection with minimal symptoms such as: fevers, cough, running nose and even rash. A single dose of 0.5 ml of reconstituted freeze-dried vaccine is given intramuscularly (in the muscle). Normally, immunity develops 11 to 12 days after vaccination.

Next, a Word about how to Treat Measles

- *Management of Measles*: There is no specific treatment for measles. Antipyretics *i.e.,* medicines to control fever, bed rest and adequate fluid intake are the basic requirements. The important aspect in management is control of secondary bacterial infection by using suitable antibiotics. Complications such as: pneumonia and middle' ear infections require appropriate treatment with antibiotics. The nutritional status of the child must be maintained properly. Children who are breast-fed and unable to suck due to soreness of mouth may be fed breast milk with a spoon after expression of the same from the mothers breast. For those children who are not breast-fed, soft diets in the form of porridges can be given. Children suffering from measles lose considerable weight and during the recovery period weight gain is slow. Children recovering from measles should be given adequate diet to stimulate faster weight gain. The child should be fed more frequently *i.e.* 5-6 times a day. The diet should include cereals like: rice or wheat, pulses (dal) and green vegetables. The child should also be given at least one glass of milk every day. The diet should be cooked soft and preferably be fed by the mother or elder member. Other dietary considerations for management of measles discussed in unit 20, block 5 of course 1 are applicable here as well. Go through those considerations carefully.

Measles can be Summarize as follows:

- Measles, an acute communicable disease is an important public health problem.
- It is caused by measles virus.
- It spreads through droplets or direct contact with secretions from nose, throat or urine of persons infected with measles.

- The disease has an incubation period of about 10 days.
- The simplest and best method to prevent measles is vaccination.
- Treatment of secondary infections and complications is the best way to manage measles.
- Maintain the nutritional status of the child by providing good nutritious food.

TUBERCULOSIS

Tuberculosis is a common disease that is found almost everywhere. It is important as a cause of disability and death in many parts of the world. In developing countries such as: India, you should expect a higher prevalence of tuberculosis in the under five age group, as a result, of greater opportunities of exposure to the disease. In other words, it is likely to occur more frequently in this age group. It is estimated that there would be atleast 9-10 million cases of pulmonary (lung) tuberculosis as well.

The Disease – What Causes It? Who gets it? How and When does it Spread?

Tuberculosis is caused by *Mycobacterium tuberculosis*, a non-motile, slender, acid-fast bacillus. Two strains – human and bovine – are of importance to man. Human source is responsible for the vast majority of Cases of India. The bacillus can be seen by examination of sputum or other secretions under a microscope after using appropriate staining procedures.

Who gets the Disease?

- *Age:* Tuberculosis can occur at any age. Recent surveys in India show that it occurs more in older age groups than the younger groups.
- *Sex:* In India, tuberculosis is more prevalent among males over 45 years of age than among females. In females however, the peak prevalence is below 35 years.
- *Socio-economic Factors:* The disease occurs more frequently in families belonging to low income groups. In Western countries a decline in death rates clue to tuberculosis has

occurred with an increase in standard of living. Communities living in substandard houses which are ill ventilated and have inadequate floor space are likely to suffer more from the disease. Miners and textiles workers are more prone to disease. Overcrowding as in the slum areas of the cities helps in the rapid spread of the disease.

Certain social customs such as: indiscriminate spitting, smoking of hukka, purdah system also help in the spread of the infection. Tuberculosis has a social stigma. This attitude leads to concealment of the disease and consequent delay in diagnosis of cases with increased risk of spreading the disease to others. Suffering from severe forms of malnutrition, almost always, they would tell you that the children had measles in the recent past. Because of loss of appetite and severe diarrhoea, the children recovering from the measles often develop severe forms of malnutrition.

Tuberculin Test is undertaken to detect tuberculosis. What is the test and how it administered is discussed below:

- *Tuberculin Test:* Persons infected with tuberculosis will react to a low dose of tuberculin test. One of the tests is Mantoux intradermal test. This is the most widely used and found satisfactory for epidemiological studies. Into the superficial layers of the skin, 0.1 mi of a standard dilution of old tuberculin (OT) or purified protein derivative (PPD) is injected. Special syringes are used for the purpose. If you notice induration (slight hardening, reddish in colour) of more than 6 mm in diameter after 72 hours, it is considered a positive test. The reaction may be negative in critically ill tuberculosis patients and during certain infectious diseases such as: measles.

Extra-pulmonary (other than lung) tuberculosis is much less common than the tuberculosis of the lungs. It includes tuberculosis meningitis (infection of the protective covering of the spinal cord), involvement of bones and joints, intestines kidneys, larynx (voice box) etc. Diagnosis is by recovery of tubercle bacilli from lesions or secretions from these lesions.

Prevention and Management of Tuberculosis

Tuberculosis can be prevented by adopting the following measures:

(a) *Improvement of Social Conditions:* Conditions which increase risk of becoming infected with tuberculosis such as: overcrowding should be removed. Housing which has proper ventilation (allowing proper light and air) should be provided particularly to the poorer communities. You may be aware that in every city, the Government has been undertaking construction of a large number of well-planned lowcost houses to rehabilitate the poor like the slum dwellers. Such steps could help in the control of tuberculosis.

The community should be educated about the mode of spread of the disease (to avoid indiscriminate spitting in public places) and motivated to seek medical advice early in case of any prolonged fever, cough, loss of appetite etc.

(b) *Early Detection and Treatment:* You can prevent and control tuberculosis by detecting early all the case of tuberculosis *i.e.,* in the initial stages of infection and providing prompt treatment. But, for diagnosis of the patients you require medical and laboratory facilities for examination of the patients. It is also important that all the family members who would have been in close contact with a tuberculosis patient and all those suspected of having tuberculosis should also be examined carefully. For this medical and laboratory facilities for tuberculin test and microscopic examination of sputum should be made available. In addition facilities for prompt treatment of all the positive cases should be provided.

(c) *BCG Vaccination:* Vaccination of uninfected (tuberculin negative) confers variable protection. It is particularly recommended to prevent infantile tuberculosis. Some controlled trials indicate that protection against tuberculosis after BCG vaccination may last for 12 years. Recent studies in India indicate that it is not very effective in preventing adult tuberculosis. In India, BCG is given to infants around the age of 3 months.

Elimination of tubemulosis among dairy cattle, tuberculin testing of the cattle and slaughter of reactors to the test and pasteurisation of milk help in preventing bovine tuberculosis.

- *Management of Tuberculosis:* Most primary infections are often inapparent and heal without treatment. When primary infection is diagnosed in children anti-tuberculosis therapy with the drug Isoniazid reduces the risk of the disease progressing further.

Patients suffering from pulmonary tuberculosis should be given prompt treatment with an appropriate combination of antimicrobial drugs for a minimum of twelve months. Current accepted regimens include using a combination of drugs like: Isoniazid, Ethambutol, Streptomycin and Paraamino Salicylic Acid (PAS). Rifampicin is recommended for resistant cases *i.e.,* those not responding to the above regimen of treatments.

How does it Spread?

Tuberculosis is transmitted by droplets from sputum of infected persons particularly during coughing. To carry infection, the droplet particles must be fresh to carry a viable organism (organism that can thrive). Prolonged household exposure to an active tuberculosis case may lead to infection of those persons in contact with such cases. Tuberculosis is not transmitted by fomites *i.e.,* dishes and other articles used by patient. Sterilization of these articles is of lime or no value.

Bovine tuberculosis results from ingestion of unpasteurised milk or dairy products of tuberculosis cows.

Primarily man and in some areas also diseased cattle are the reservoir of infection of tuberculosis.

- *Incubation Period:* It takes about 4-12 weeks from the time an individual is infected from an active case of tuberculosis to demonstrable primary lesion. It may take years to lead to progressive pulmonary or extra-pulmonary, tuberculosis. You should remember that tuberculosis infection means entry or development of the organism M. tuberculosis, while the disease has specific manifestations (symptoms and signs) resulting from the infection.

- *Period of Communicability:* The disease is communicable *i.e.,* can spread from a patient of tuberculosis to a non-infected individual, as long as tubercle bacilli are discharged by the patient. Some untreated, as in the poorer communities, or inadequately treated (discontinuing treatment patients may be intermittently sputum positive for years. In other words, there is a constant danger of getting the disease from such patients. Proper treatment generally reduces communicability within a few weeks, it only means that for control of tuberculosis, prompt and complete treatment 'are essential. Extra-pulmonary tuberculosis without any discharge (secretions) is not directly communicable.
- *Susceptibility:* Everyone is susceptible to the disease. However, children under the age of 3 years are highly susceptible. In undernourished individuals susceptibility is high. Susceptibility is lowest in later childhood *i.e.* 4-10 years, but is again high in adolescents and young adults.

Symptoms and Complications

Tuberculosis is a chronic disease, *i.e.,* a disease of gradual onset and long duration. The primary infection, in young children, usually goes unnoticed clinically. The primary tuberculosis lesions (pathological changes in tissues) commonly become inactive leaving no residual changes. However, it may also progress to active pulmonary (lung) tuberculosis and further spread through lympho-haematogenous (blood) path to involve the nervous system, particularly the meninges (membranous coverings of brain and spinal cord).

Palmonary tuberculosis, is characterised by a variable and often a symptomatic (symptomless) course with exacerabations (increase in severity) and remissions (abatement of symptoms). Clinically, it is confirmed by presence of tubercle bacilli in sputum (matter ejected from lungs, trachea and bronchi through mouth). Abnormal X-Ray densities indicative of pulmonary involvement occur before clinical manifestations (clinical signs and symptoms). The patients may have cough, easy fatiguability (gets tired with little effort), fever, loss of weight and appetite, hoarseness of voice, and chest pain. The patient may bring out blood in sputum, particularly in advanced stages, Most often, the patient, usually from a low income family, presents himself before a doctor in advanced stage.

Sputum examination by direct microscopy is now considered the method of choice for finding out cases of tuberculosis. Under Indian Tuberculosis control programme micro-scope examination of sputum is performed as a routine on patients who attend hospitals and primary health centres with the following chest symptoms:

1. Cough lasting for more than 4 weeks.
2. Continuous fever.
3. Chest pain.
4. Blood in sputum.

Proper Diet Plays a Helping Role in Controlling the Disease

Recent advances encourage treatment of patients at their homes under domiciliary management of tuberculosis. Under the scheme the patients hake medicines prescribed by specialists at their houses continuously without need for hospitalisation. This reduces the cost of treatment quite substantially. However, the patients should be educated and motivated to complete the treatment and not to discontinue the treatment as soon as there is improvement in the general conditions of the patient.

WHOOPING COUGH

Whooping cough is an acute highly communicable infection of the respiratory tract. The Chinese call it a hundred day cough – because it is a disease which lasts for about 3 months or more. In India and other developing countries, it is still a serious disease accounting for considerable number of deaths among children. It also leads to complications. In infants (under one year of age) 4-15 per cent of cases of whooping cough end in deaths.

The Disease – What Causes it? Who gets it? How and When does it Spread?

Whooping cough is caused by micro-organism *Bordetella pertussis or* the *Pertussia bacillus.* In about 5 per cent of the cases *B. paraperttssia* is the causative organism. In such cases the disease is milder. Certain viruses also can cause a similar clinical synchrome.

Who gets the Disease?

- *Age:* It is primarily a disease of infants and children. The disease is considered as a pediatric priority. In other words, it is considered as an important disease of children. In countries such as: India about 50 per cent of the cases occur between 20-30 months of age. In the developed counaies of the west, however, it occurs around the age of 50 months. The death rates are the highest below the age of one year.
- *Sex:* The disease affects both males and females equally. But the mortality is observed to be higher among girls as compared to boys.
- *Socio-economic Factors:* The disease takes a serious form in malnourished children. Such children who are already weak do not have resistance to any disease. Similarly, in communities which are poor and exposed to multiple infections, whooping cough is a lethal disease of children. In these communities, children who are already exposed to other infections like: diarrhoea etc., will be weak and whooping cough may take a severe form and lead to death.

How does it Spread?

The disease is spread mainly by droplet infection, like most of the respiratory tract infections, and also by direct contact. Each time, the patient of whooping cough talks, coughs or sneezes the causative organisms (pertusis bacilli) are sprayed into the air. If a susceptible person is within the range of the spray of droplets, he is likely to inhale the same. Most children contract the infection from their playmates during the early stages of the disease.

Similarly, direct contact with discharges from respiratory tract of infected cases (sputum, nasal discharges) can spread the disease. Indirect contact with oxticles freshly soiled with the discharges of infected persons also contribute to the transmission of the disease.

- *Incubation Period:* Normally, it takes about 7-10 days for a child to get infected from the time of exposure to an infected person. It is never beyond 3 weeks.
- *Period of Communicability:* The disease is highly communicable during the initial catarrhal stage (during the stage of slight cough with running nose) before the child develops typical paroxysmal cough. The communicability of the disease become negligible in about 3 weeks. The period of infectiousness extends only 5-7 days after starting of treatment with appropriate antibiotics. In other words, prompt treatment reduces the infectivity of the disease and reduces spread of the disease.
- *Susceptibility:* Every individual, particularly under the age of 7 years of age is susceptible to the disease. Numerous cases of infection without any clinical manifestations or a typical case can occur. This means that in several children the disease is mild and passes off as an ordinary respiratory infection.

Symptoms and Complications

Whooping cough begins with a slight cough, usually accompanied by running nose. The cough then assumes a firequency which is out of proportion with the thin discharge from the nose. Usually, coughs associated with colds with thin discharge from the nose are of milder nature. In the case of whooping cough, however, you would notice that it is of severe degree. Within 1-2 weeks, the cough comes in bursts and the child with whooping cough, unlike the child with bronchitis, does not take a breath in anticipation of the burst of coughing. At the end of the second week, the coughing spasms increase in speed, rise in pitch, and the paroxysms become longer and more intense. The cough is characterised by high pitched crowing or inspiratory whoop (a peculiar sound while breathing in). Hence, it is called whooping cough. The rapid spasmodic cough is generally associated with choking and vomiting, with the production of sticky sputum. In the case of young infants and adults the typical whoop may be absent.

The chief complications are broncho-pneumonia and severe bronchitis. The severe paroxysmal cough may sometimes lead to bleeding under the conjunctiva (white portion) of the eye or bleeding through nose. The children may develop convulsions (fits) and go into coma (deep unconsciousness).

There is considerable evidence flint whooping cough may lead to severe malnutrition The children are liable to poor weight gain and end up in marasmus – a nutritional disorder due to protein energy malnutrition-characterised by extreme muscular wasting. Hence, proper nutritional care is necessary during convalescence.

Prevention and Management

The following measures can prevent whooping cough:

1. *Active Immunisation:* An effective vaccine is now available for protection against the disease. The vaccine is given one at the age of 1 1/2 to 2 years and another at 5 years of age. It is generally given along with diphtheria and tetanus toxoids as a triple vaccine or DPT vaccine.
2. *Education: The* parents of/he infants should be educated about the dangers of the disease, particularly in young children, and encouraged to get their infants immunised. The Government of India have now launched a massive education programme through mass media such as: Doordarshan and All India Radio to educate the communities about, the importance of immunisation.
3. *Isolation of Cases:* Known cases of whooping cough should be isolated and wherever possible susceptible children (not immunised and not affected by the disease so far) should be excluded· and exempted from schools and public places for 14 days after last exposure to a household case of whooping cough. This would help in reducing the spread of the disease by them if they also get infected.

Management of Whooping cough is simple. The measures adopted are discussed below:

- *Management of Whooping Cough:* Erythromycin or Ampicillin drug is used in infants and children as the specific treatment for whooping cough.

Points to Remember given below lists the salient features of whooping cough.

Whooping cough can be summarize as follows:

- Whooping cough is an acute highly communicable infection of the respiratory tract.
- It is caused by micro-organism *Bordetella pertussis* or *pertussis bacillus.*
- Infants and children are more prone to whooping cough.
- The infection spreads by droplet and direct contact.
- The incubation period for the disease is 7-10 days.
- Burst of cough associated with cold and thin discharge from the nose are the symptoms of the disease.
- Complications of the disease are broncho-pneumonia and severe bronchitis.
- The simplest and the best way to prevent whooping cough is through active immunisation.

Bibliography

1. Ahmed and Coelho (1979). Toward a New Definition of Health, Plenum, N.Y., London.
2. Bamji, M.S. (1989). Medicine Digest, 9(12) 5-14.
3. Benerji (1985). Health and Family Planning Services in India, Lok Paksh, New Delhi.
4. Bhat, R. (1977). Nutrition, July 1977, Hyderabad.
5. Bourne, GH (1971). World Review of Nutrition and Dietetics, Vol. 13, p. 106-164, Karger Basel.
6. Crew (1965). Health Its Nature and Conservation, Pergamon Press London.
7. Dubos, R. (1968). Man, Med and Environment, Hammond Sport, Pelican.
8. Donald, C.A. (1978). Social Health in Conceptualization and Measurement of Health for Adults in the Health Insurance Study, Santa Monica CA, and Corporation Vol. 4.
9. Evang, K. (1967). Health of Mankind, Ciba Foundation. 100th Symposium, Churchill.
10. Falkner. F ed. (1980). Preservation in Childhood of Health Problems in Adult Life, WHO.
11. Government of India, (1986). Health Information of India, Central Bureau of Health Intelligence, DGHS, Nirman Bhawan, New Delhi.

12. Gopalan, C. and Kamala J.R. (1980). In: Preservation in Childhood of Health Problem in Adult Life, Geneva.
13. Gopalan C. (1980). Nutrition and Health Care, Nutrition Foundation of India, Spl. Pub. No. 1.
14. Gopalan C. *et.al.*, (1989). Nutrition Value of Indian Foods, National Institute of Nutrition Hyderabad.
15. Hetzel, B.S. (1985). In: Oxford Textbook of Public Health, Vol. 4, p. 28.
16. Indian Council of Social Science Research and ICMR (1981). Health for all An Alternative Strategy Voluntary Asso. of India New Delhi.
17. ICMR (1980). Nutritive Value of Indian Foods, National Institute of Nutrition, Hyderabad.
18. Layrisse, M. *et.al.* (1976). Nutrition in Preventive Medicine, WHO Monograph No. 62.
19. Mohan Ram and I Gopalan (1981). Nutritional Disabilities ICMR, National Institution of Nutrition Hyderabad.
20. National Institute of Nutrition (1975). Nutrition, October, 1975, Hyderabad.
21. Nagpal, R. and Sell H. (1985). Subjective Well-being, Reg. Health Paper No. 7 SEARO. WHO New Delhi.
22. Narsinga Rao, B.S (1986). Nutrition, 20 (1) 14.
23. Pandit. C.G. *et.al.* (1960). Nutrition in India New Delhi, ICMR.
24. Passmore, R. *et.al.* (1974). Handbook on Human Nutritional Requirements, Geneva.
25. Rodricks, J.V. (1976) Food Nutrition (FAO) 2:9.
26. Ramadasmurthy V. and M. Mohanram (1984). Your Nutrition and Health, N.I.N. Hyderabad.
27. Shah P.M. (1974). Early Detection and Prevention of Protein – Caloric Malnutrition Popular Prakasan, Bombay.
28. Swaminathan M. (1983). Human Nutrition and Diet. The Banglore Printing and Publication Col. Ltd. Banglore.
29. Swaminathan, M. (1974). Essentials of Food and Nutrition, Ganesh and Co. Madras 17.

30. Tasher, T. (1986). Food and Nutrition, Bulletin, 8 (13) 12.
31. Who (1986). Concepts of Health Behaviour Research, Reg. Health Paper No. 13 SEARO, New Delhi.
32. WHO (1975). Promoting Health in the Human Environment, Geneva.
33. WHO (1981). Health for all, Sr. No. 6.
34. Wilson, R. W. and T. F. Drury (1984). Ann. Rev. Public Health. 5:83-106.
35. WHO (1979). The Health Aspects of Food and Nutrition, Manila.

Index

❑❑❑